THE NEXT DAY

TRAVASA HOLLOWAY-BUFORD

TNHB Inspirations, LLC
Mobile, Alabama

THE NEXT DAY

Published by
TNHB Inspirations, LLC
tnhb.inspirations@yahoo.com

Travasa Buford, Publisher
Yvonne Rose/Oualitypress.info-Book Packager
Editorial Services –VoiceVessel Publications, LLC
Photo courtesy of Julia Kristman, Julia Alayna Photography
Front and Back Cover Design courtesy of Rodney Goldsmith,
Graphic ENT.

Another Day Has Finally Come Poem appears courtesy of VoiceVessel
Publications, LLC
All scripture references courtesy of (NLV) Bible
All quotes have been identified by author.

All Rights Reserved

No part of this book may be reproduced or transmitted in any form or by any means, unless permission is obtained by the author.

The content is for informational and inspirational purposes only and does not take place of any medical or professional consultations.

Copyright © 2018 by Travasa Buford
ISBN #: 978-0-578-41336-5
Library of Congress Control Number: 2018914205

DEDICATION

I dedicate this writing journey to my daddy Charles "Hutley" "Hollywood" Holloway, uncle/brother Kenneth "Kenny" "Cool H" Holloway and granddaddy James Watson "JW" Peden

I've learned what real men look like through you all.

Your spirit lives on through me.

ACKNOWLEDGEMENTS

Every day, I thank God for continuing to provide, uplift and keep me. He continues to refresh me, even when my thoughts are consumed with just walking away and giving up. However, without hesitation, my Heavenly Father continues to pour His Word into me daily. That way, I can encourage others who might be experiencing the same trials and tribulations. Meanwhile, as I'm encouraging others, He sends mighty prayer warriors to encompass me with a word, and for that I am grateful.

With love, I thank you and I love you to life.

Ra'Mon & Rod Holloway
Pastor Rabon L. & Mia Turner
Pastor Tyshawn & Shonetay Gardner
Dr. Derrol & Patricia H. Dawkins
Pastor Leroy & Tina Caudle
Bishop Daniel J. & Tiffany Richardson
Minister Sonya Drake
Mother Katherine Floyd
Family & Friends

CONTENTS

Dedication --- i
Acknowledgements -- iii
Contents--- v
Introduction -- xxi
The next day--- xxii
January 1: "I" "I" & I -------------------------------------- 1
January 2: Second Chances --------------------------------- 2
January 3: Strong, But Exhausted ------------------------- 3
January 4: Stop Giving Your Pearls to Swine ------------- 4
January 5: But I Can't Pray --------------------------------- 5
January 6: Seeing Your Rainbow --------------------------- 6
January 7: Calm vs. Rage ----------------------------------- 7
January 8: Where Are You God? --------------------------- 8
January 9: The Path --- 9
January 10: Cheers --- 10
January 11: Do the Thing You Think You Can't --------- 11
January 12: Right Now Isn't Forever ---------------------- 12
January 13: Prodigious Strength -------------------------- 13
January 14: Doubt Your Doubt --------------------------- 14
January 15: A Dead Fish & A Live Fish ------------------- 15
January 16: Build Your Muscle Up ----------------------- 16
January 17: Let the Air Out of Your Balloon ------------ 17
January 18: Impressing the Bird & Horse --------------- 18
January 19: The Thought of It ---------------------------- 19
January 20: It's Not Too Far ------------------------------ 20

January 21: Stronger Than You Think --------------------------------------- 21
January 22: Progress is Impossible Without Change ---------------------- 22
January 23: Standing Tall -- 23
January 24: Tie A Knot and Hold On ------------------------------------- 24
January 25: You Are What You Eat -- 25
January 26: By Perseverance You Can ------------------------------------ 26
January 27: Serve Notice to The Enemy --------------------------------- 27
January 28: Gossip & Verbal Defamation -------------------------------- 28
January 29: Getting Beat Down -- 29
January 30: A Bird, Worm & Nest --- 30
January 31: Forget About It --- 31

February 1: Everything is Out of Control --------------------------------- 32
February 2: Take Your Cues from God ----------------------------------- 33
February 3: No Pressure, No Diamonds ---------------------------------- 34
February 4: But I'm Worried About It ------------------------------------- 35
February 5: A Loss & A Gain --- 36
February 6: So What...They Left -- 37
February 7: I've Been Suffering For Too Long ------------------------- 38
February 8: Have Enough Sense To Walk Away ---------------------- 39
February 9: It's In Perfect Order --- 40
February 10: God Has A Better One -------------------------------------- 41
February 11: How Are You Behaving? ------------------------------------ 42
February 12: Check Yourself -- 43
February 13: A Promise Keeper -- 44
February 14: YES! It's Valentine's Day ------------------------------------ 45
February 15: Stop Touching It --- 46

February 16: It's Too Expensive --- 47

February 17: God's In Charge -- 48

February 18: Change Your World With Your Words ----------------------- 49

February 19: Forgive Your Enemy --- 50

February 20: You Sin Too --- 51

February 21: Good Riddance --- 52

February 22: Drinking Tears For Water ------------------------------------- 53

February 23: Change The Chord in Your Voice ---------------------------- 54

February 24: The Best Speech You Will Ever Regret ---------------------- 55

February 25: Free Your Mind --- 56

February 26: Poison --- 57

February 27: Keep Riding Your Bicycle ------------------------------------- 58

February 28: You Have to Face It -- 59

March 1: It's Going To Cost You --- 60

March 2: How Are You Going To React? ------------------------------------ 61

March 3: Be Calm While You Wait --- 62

March 4: No Enemy Within --- 63

March 5: Now What -- 64

March 6: You're Doing The Wrong Thing ----------------------------------- 65

March 7: When Are You Going To Begin ----------------------------------- 66

March 8: Stressful Thinking -- 67

March 9: When Trouble Comes Back For An Encore ---------------------- 68

March 10: Stop Watering Concrete -- 69

March 11: Zip It!!! -- 70

March 12: This Will Be One Day As If It Never Was ----------------------- 71

March 13: What Happened To You? --- 72

March 14: I Don't Mean No Harm.... BUT --- 73

March 15: Strong Enough To Stand Up Again --- 74

March 16: What's The Story You're Telling Yourself? --- 75

March 17: Use The Bricks Thrown At You --- 76

March 18: Your Mirror is Being Polished --- 77

March 19: Complaining of A Headache --- 78

March 20: But You Gave Them Access --- 79

March 21: You've Survived A Lot --- 80

March 22: You're Asking The Wrong Questions --- 81

March 23: The Mistake You Made --- 82

March 24: The Leaves Aren't Worried --- 83

March 25: You Made it...Now Lie in It!!! --- 84

March 26: "F" -- You Failed! --- 85

March 27: This is Not What I Wanted --- 86

March 28: The Truth or A Lie --- 87

March 29: Stop Raising The Dead!!!! --- 88

March 30: The Trial of My Life --- 89

March 31: Stuck in The Corner --- 90

April 1: And This is How You Treat Me --- 91

April 2: Time & Karma --- 92

April 3: Who Cares? I'm ANGRY --- 93

April 4: You Failed, Now What? --- 94

April 5: A Ruined Future --- 95

April 6: But I Want To Go NOW --- 96

April 7: Stop Letting Trifles Disturb Your Tranquility --- 97

April 8: Fakes & Frauds Are Unqualified --- 98

April 9: The Next Time You Open Your Mouth — 99
April 10: YOU Need To STOP — 100
April 11: Your Mind is Your Own Mirror — 101
April 12: The Enemy Has You Right Where God Wants You — 102
April 13: Big Trees Out of Small Seeds — 103
April 14: Diluting Your Truth — 104
April 15: Some Bridges Need to Be Burned — 105
April 16: The Right to Remain Silent — 106
April 17: He Can't Lie — 107
April 18: Cheers to My Problems — 108
April 19: With Every Good Deed You Are Sowing A Seed — 109
April 20: Who is Really in Your Way? — 110
April 21: I Got A Bully — 111
April 22: This Is Like A Fairy Tale — 112
April 23: Be a Kite — 113
April 25: The Thief of Time — 114
April 26: The Wolf Really Ain't That Big — 115
April 27: Deuces — 116
April 28: What's on The Inside? — 117
April 29: Running Out of Gas — 118
April 30: A Blackout — 119

May 1: OMG!!! What Am I Going To Do? — 120
May 2: Do You Really Think That's a Good Idea? — 121
May 3: Some Changes Look Negative — 122
May 4: Stormy Weather — 123
May 5: Don't Burn Your Opportunities For A Temporary Comfort — 124

May 6: Bag Lady, Bag Man --- 125
May 7: Why Do I Have To Go Through This? ---------------------------- 126
May 8: It Doesn't Make it Right --- 127
May 9: You Can't Cross The Sea by Staring   at The Water -------------- 128
May 10: That Tongue of Yours is The Enemy of The Soul -------------- 129
May 11: A Difficult Exam -- 130
May 12: Why Are You Always Picking on Me? --------------------------- 131
May 13: It Had to Take All That --- 132
May 14: What I Did, What I Didn't Do, & What I Should've Done -------- 133
May 15: But I Gotta Say it --- 134
May 16: You Have Nothing to Be Ashamed About --------------------- 135
May 17: Buried Alive --- 136
May 18: Let Em' Keep Touching The Stove ------------------------------ 137
May 19: Out of My Control -- 138
May 20: An Extraordinary Move of God --------------------------------- 139
May 21: Prepare a Victory Speech --------------------------------------- 140
May 22: The Blueprint --- 141
May 23: You're Still Valuable --- 142
May 24: Don't Let Your Gift Take You
Where Your Character Won't Keep You ---------------------------------- 143
May 25: You're Too Familiar with The Word Impossible ---------------- 144
May 26: I Think I Can, I Think I Can -------------------------------------- 145
May 27: He Orders Your STOPS Too ------------------------------------- 146
May 28: Current Conditions -- 147
May 29: I Wish I Would Have --- 148
May 30: All Night Long -- 149
May 31: It Wasn't Meant For You -- 150

June 1: The Hell of Unhappiness --- 151
June 2: A Purpose Before They Had an Opinion --- 152
June 3: I'm Not Going to Jail --- 153
June 4: Everybody's Afraid of Something --- 154
June 5: It's Okay...HE Hears YOU --- 155
June 6: Aiding and Abetting --- 156
June 7: This Isn't Your Stop --- 157
June 8: Stop Talking About How Bad You Feel --- 158
June 9: You Don't Have to Like Me --- 159
June 10: Stop Chasing Folks That Don't Want You --- 160
June 11: A Matter of Personal Taste --- 161
June 12: But I Wanna Smack Em --- 162
June 13: Pepsi or Coke --- 163
June 14: Are You Gonna Get Ugly With Yourself? --- 164
June 15: I Want it My Way --- 165
June 16: This is Drowning Me --- 166
June 17: A Temporary Condition --- 167
June 18: The Grudge --- 168
June 19: Stop Biting the Bait --- 169
June 20: Sacrificing Your Peace --- 170
June 21: A Worst Situation --- 171
June 22: This is Bothering Me --- 172
June 23: I've Been Injured --- 173
June 24: A Broken Wing --- 174
June 25: Thank God it Didn't Work --- 175
June 26: My Back is Breaking --- 176
June 27: I Got Weeds in My Garden --- 177

June 28: They're Not Always Dressed The Way You Think --------------- 178
June 29: A Bird Doesn't Compete With A Plane ---------------------------- 179
June 30: You Too Will Get Out of Oz -- 180

July 1: It Doesn't Matter How You Feel ------------------------------------- 181
July 2: But They Won't Forgive You --- 182
July 3: I Can't Live Without It --- 183
July 4: You Failed To Heal From It --- 184
July 5: The Consequences --- 185
July 6: It's Ruining Everything -- 186
July 7: Don't Forget To Take Your Vitamins ------------------------------- 187
July 8: Comfort To Discomfort To Greater Comfort ---------------------- 188
July 9: Don't Be a Bird of a Feather --------------------------------------- 189
July 10: Don't Stop Praying --- 190
July 11: This Can't Be Final --- 191
July 12: The Past is a Place of Learning ---------------------------------- 192
July 13: Don't Let The Devil Steal Your Shout --------------------------- 193
July 14: This is How I See It --- 194
July 15: They Think I'm Crazy -- 195
July 16: Why Are You Calling Me Lord Then? ---------------------------- 196
July 17: If You Can Get Through THAT, You Can Get Through THIS ---- 197
July 18: Smile! Even On The Worst Days --------------------------------- 198
July 19: I'm Going To Avoid It --- 199
July 20: You're Responsible For Your Future ----------------------------- 200
July 21: A Box Full of Chocolates -- 201
July 22: Give The Gift of Absence --- 202
July 23: ....And You Will Never Have -------------------------------------- 203

July 24: I Can't! I'm Scared --- 204
July 25: Ships Are Safe in The Harbor --- 205
July 26: Act Like You Already Won --- 206
July 27: I Don't Feel Anything --- 207
July 28: Move Your Feet --- 208
July 29: Watch Me --- 209
July 30: You Can & You Will --- 210
July 31: Nothing Just Happens --- 211

August 1: Stop Thinking About It --- 212
August 2: The Worst Time of My Life --- 213
August 3: The Curve Ball Thrown --- 214
August 4: Tortoise & The Hare --- 215
August 5: But I Fell Down Yesterday --- 216
August 6: It's Not Three Strikes --- 217
August 7: Who Are You to Judge --- 218
August 8: The Attack is Proof --- 219
August 9: Whateva --- 220
August 10: You Can't Be Beat --- 221
August 11: Powerful Praise from A Person in Pain --- 222
August 12: Cool More Than Cold Water --- 223
August 13: You're A Great Peach --- 224
August 14: Who's Going to Stop You? --- 225
August 15: Soldiers Triumph in War --- 226
August 16: Maybe You're The Reason --- 227
August 17: An Entry Somewhere Else --- 228
August 18: I Don't Feel Like It --- 229

August 19: Lean Not To Thy Own Understanding --------------------------230
August 20: Imagination vs. Reality--231
August 21: An Idiot Will Persist ---232
August 22: The Greatest Disappointment-------------------------------233
August 23: Your Ride or Die---234
August 24: You're Being Polished --235
August 25: How Are You? I'm Fine! ---------------------------------------236
August 26: Are You Wearing Your Heartache Like Thorns? -------------237
August 27: I'm Tired of Doing the Right Thing--------------------------238
August 28: Being Eliminated---239
August 29: You're Somebody's Answered Prayers----------------------240
August 30: This Stress is Killing Me---------------------------------------241
August 31: Act Like You Can't Fail --242

September 1: The Best Revenge---243
September 2: Rock YOU --244
September 3: The Echoes in Eternity------------------------------------245
September 4: Seeing Yourself ---246
September 5: Intimidated & Terrorized, But Survived ----------------247
September 6: You're Not Sinking --248
September 7: The Strength For It--249
September 8: Counting The Blessings or Problems --------------------250
September 9: Start Making Some Adjustments --------------------------251
September 10: But I Want Something Better----------------------------252
September 11: Getting Comfortable in the Uncomfortable --------------253
September 12: Stop Arguing With Them--------------------------------254
September 13: Stop Letting Them Get To You ----------------------------255

September 14: But What Do You See --- 256
September 15: It's Time To Get Dirty --- 257
September 16: Act Like You Have Risen --- 258
September 17: I'm Drowning --- 259
September 18: Signaling For Help --- 260
September 19: I Don't Look Like What I've Been Through --- 261
September 20: Who is Writing Your Script --- 262
September 21: The Worry of Today, Yesterday & Tomorrow --- 263
September 22: Accept the Loss --- 264
September 23: Stop Going Back on Your Word --- 265
September 24: The Two Thieves in Your Life --- 266
September 25: Stop Watching the Clock --- 267
September 26: Keep Being Ignorant or Be Wise --- 268
September 27: I Need --- 269
September 28: What's the Excuse Now --- 270
September 29: What Are You Going To Say? --- 271
September 30: Don't Worry, It Will Come Back --- 272

October 1: Are You Correcting or Encouraging --- 273
October 2: The Authority in Your Silence --- 274
October 3: My Hero --- 275
October 4: You Was Taught Better Than That --- 276
October 5: Thank You For The Experience --- 277
October 6: The Secret for Changing Your Future --- 278
October 7: Unnecessary Suffering --- 279
October 8: Is This The End? --- 280
October 9: A Sudden Impact --- 281

October 10: Reacting or Deciding --282
October 11: A River Cuts Through Rocks --------------------------------283
October 12: "The Memory" (Was it True or False)------------------------284
October 13: Failed Plans NOT Failed Visions ---------------------------285
October 14: God's Promise or Your Wants?------------------------------286
October 15: The Distance Between Problems ---------------------------287
October 16: Stop Running Around Like A Firefighter?------------------288
October 17: Things Are Moving Slow--289
October 18: Work Never Killed Anyone --------------------------------290
October 19: Little Hinges Swing Big Doors-------------------------------291
October 20: Your Speed is Increasing --------------------------------292
October 21: It's Not the End of The World----------------------------293
October 22: Your Dream is Still Alive---------------------------------294
October 23: A Learned Fool Vs. An Ignorant Fool --------------------295
October 24: YOU Are More Than Your Name--------------------------296
October 25: You Can't Hear, Because You Talk Too Much--------------297
October 26: Truth Will Always Be Truth ------------------------------298
October 27: It's Not About the Size of The Dog----------------------299
October 28: Their Opinion is NOT Your Reality ---------------------300
October 29: It Should Be Common Sense ---------------------------301
October 30: Are You Living Your Fears or Dreams --------------------302
October 31: It Must Start With YOU -----------------------------------303

November 1: The Tool in Your Hand ----------------------------------304
November 2: There is Consequences to Acting a Fool ----------------305
November 3: Did it Defeat YOU or Did You Defeat IT? ---------------306
November 4: It's The Fear That's Killing You -----------------------307

November 5: You Weren't Always Saved --- 308
November 6: You Actually Won --- 309
November 7: Would You Want It Done To You? --- 310
November 8: I Want it and I Want it NOW --- 311
November 9: You Really Didn't Lose --- 312
November 10: It's Disrupting Your Present --- 313
November 11: It Lies Within You --- 314
November 12: Who Said Something is Wrong with You? --- 315
November 13: Watch What You Plant --- 316
November 14: I'm Broke and Poor --- 317
November 15: They're Acting a Complete Fool --- 318
November 16: It's Only Impossible for a Fool --- 319
November 17: Stop the Madness --- 320
November 18: There is Only One-Way Around --- 321
November 19: Who Said It's Wrong? --- 322
November 20: What if They Knew? --- 323
November 21: Defending A Lie --- 324
November 22: The Situation --- 325
November 23: Selective Kindness --- 326
November 24: You Don't Owe an Explanation --- 327
November 25: Start Digging Two Graves --- 328
November 26: I Hate My Past --- 329
November 27: If Your Scars Could Talk --- 330
November 28: You Don't Need Anyone's Permission --- 331
November 29: Fix Your Attitude --- 332
November 30: This is Embarrassing Me --- 333

December 1: Don't Go Broke in This Season --- 334
December 2: I Need Olivia Pope --- 335
December 3: Who Said It Was Going To Make Sense? --- 336
December 4: The Company You Keep --- 337
December 5: I Might --- 338
December 6: Poor Choices --- 339
December 7: Be What You're Looking For --- 340
December 8: Stay Miserable Then --- 341
December 9: What is My Character Saying? --- 342
December 10: It Broke My Heart --- 343
December 11: Trying to Prove a Point --- 344
December 12: Which Cat Are You Copying? --- 345
December 13: Justice --- 346
December 14: Let Them Remain Fools --- 347
December 15: The Wrong Train --- 348
December 16: The Inevitable and The Choice --- 349
December 17: Who Are You in The Dark? --- 350
December 18: A Rocking Chair --- 351
December 19: Crossing Monkey Bars --- 352
December 20: At The End of This --- 353
December 21: God Don't Change --- 354
December 22: Yesterday's Junk --- 355
December 23: Tired of Rejection --- 356
December 24: Temporary Pleasure, But Permanent Regret --- 357
December 25: It's More Than Christmas Presents --- 358
December 26: Folks Keep Letting Me Down --- 359
December 27: Do The Right Thing --- 360

December 28: I've Run Out of Cheeks ------------------------------------ 361
December 29: Really God? -- 362
December 30: The Greatest Mistake You'll Make ----------------------- 363
December 31: It's Gorgeous At The End -------------------------------- 364
About the Author -- 365

INTRODUCTION

At the end of the day, I have lost so much. I lost my granddaddy and that crushed me. I lost my dad and that broke my heart. I lost my marriage and that almost took my life. I lost my grandmamma and that left me grief-stricken. Then I lost my beloved dog, Diva and that devastated me. Nonetheless, I know that God has strengthened me to embrace a new tomorrow. I can honestly say that at the end of the day, my season of sorrow propelled me to look forward to seeing a new day. Even though, I don't know what tomorrow may bring, I am certain that either way I'll be just fine because, I know who holds tomorrow and who allows me to embrace *The Next Day and the new season of my life.*

I invite you to journal your thoughts after reading the devotionals. My hope is that as you read you will embrace a new day by believing that *your Next Day* will be filled with an abundance of joy and hope.

THE NEXT DAY

Another Day Has Finally Come
Rising on the brink of dawn
Is the newness of opportunities being sent your way
It refreshes everything just as the dew on the morning lawn
It reminds you that the next day arrived finally after your last day
After dusk comes dawn
After rain comes sun
After night comes day
New opportunities to live, to love, to create and to forgive have been sent your way
Rising on the brink of dawn
Another Day comes
After dusk comes dawn
After rain comes sun
After night comes day
New opportunities to live, to love, to create, and to forgive have been sent your way
When it arrives may you seize the moment
Choose to no longer live in torment
Arise with the dawn
Rise from the shadows of your own heart
Embrace each breath as if you've been granted a new start
Consider you have been given another day to be freed
From whence you've already overcome
For *Another Day* has finally come
For *Another Day* has finally come

- *Shannon B. Talley*
Author, Hear My Voice and Committing Suicide to Live Again
Voice Vessel Inspirations LLC

JANUARY 1

"I" "I" & I"

"I" "I" & "I" That's all some folks know. They think that it's them that's doing it and did it.

YES! You deserve an applause. But truth is you have to humble yourself to God so you can be exalted. (1 Peter 5:6)

Remember, there is no such thing as a self-made man/woman. Somebody helped you, believed in you, prayed for you, encouraged you, counseled you, and coached you. (Bishop Dale C. Bronner)

But He gives more grace. Therefore it says, "God opposes the proud, but gives grace to the humble."" (James 4:6)

"Pride goes before destruction, and a haughty spirit before a fall." (Proverbs 16:18)

_____

_____

_____

_____

_____

_____

_____

_____

_____

_____

_____

JANUARY 2

SECOND CHANCES

Have you ever wanted to redo and get a second chance at something? But before you get that do-over, ask yourself: *What did I learn from my first mistake?*

Truth is, life is all about mistakes, learning and lessons. What you do with them determines your outcome and success.

Remember, you can get a second chance. But it doesn't and won't mean anything if you didn't learn from your mistake.

"Indeed, we all make many mistakes. For if we could control our tongues, we would be perfect and could also control ourselves in every other way." (James 3:2)

JANUARY 3

STRONG, BUT EXHAUSTED

Strong. That's a powerful word in itself. And most people become strong because they're able to withstand great force and pressure. But often when exhaustion takes control, it can make one think they're weak. But they're not!!!!

Today, no matter how you feel or what the enemy tries to do or say. You're not weak. But indeed strong!!!! (2 Corinthians 4:8-9)

Remember, just because you're strong doesn't mean you don't get exhausted. Don't confuse exhaustion for weakness. (Bishop Dale C. Bronner)

"Even young people get tired, then stumble and fall. But those who trust the LORD will find new strength. They will be strong like eagles soaring upward on wings; they will walk and run without getting

JANUARY 4

STOP GIVING YOUR PEARLS TO SWINE

You give and give. Pour out to others. Yet folks still take your kindness for weakness.

Today, stop giving your pearls away. You're precious, royal and honored. (Isaiah 43:4) Not everyone will appreciate you or your gifts.

Remember, stop giving your pearls to swine...some people will never truly appreciate your wisdom, gift or time. Even when you give it to them they don't know what to do with it. (Pastor Jamal Bryant)

"Behold, I am sending you out as sheep in the midst of wolves, so be wise as serpents and innocent as doves." (Matthew 10:16)

_____
_____
_____
_____
_____
_____
_____
_____
_____
_____
_____
_____
_____
_____

JANUARY 5

BUT I CAN'T PRAY

Life can be hard, cold and difficult to say the least. Folks are quick to keep telling you it's alright. Leave it alone and pray about it. But truth be told - you don't have it in you to even pray. Sound familiar?

Today, know that it's okay if you can't or don't want to pray. Sometimes just calling the name of JESUS, is all that it takes. (Romans 10:13)

Remember, the name Jesus is prayer by itself! (Bishop Dale C. Bronner)

"You can ask for anything in my name, and I will do it, so that the

JANUARY 6

SEEING YOUR RAINBOW

Rainbows are beautiful. But it's not like you get to see them every day. You only get to see them after it rains and an arch of colors are formed in the sky by dispersion of sunlight.

Truth is the light is shining on your situation right now, and your rainbow is coming up. All the suffering, pain, hurt and despair is not in vain. The SON is shining upon YOU!!!! (Psalms 18:28)

Remember, if something happens that causes you pain, remind yourself that you can't get the rainbow without a little rain. (RVM)

"May the LORD make his face shine on you and be gracious to you;" (Numbers 6:25)

_____
_____
_____
_____
_____
_____
_____
_____
_____
_____
_____
_____

JANUARY 7

CALM VS. RAGE

When a storm comes in your life it can come with a vengeance. Making it seem like it's going on and on. When in actuality, all you want it to do is cease and desist.

Today, know that Jesus can suddenly rebuke the storm you're in. (Mark 4:39) But He often teaches lessons while in it.

Remember, sometimes, you wait for the storm to calm. But other times, the storm will rage on, and you have to be the calm one. (T.J. Holmes)

"If a ruler's anger rises against you, do not leave your post; calmness

JANUARY 8

WHERE ARE YOU GOD?

Where are you God? Are you feeling like that lately? You've prayed. Been standing. Fasted and you continue to sow. Yet, you're feeling as if God still isn't moving in your life.

Well, just because you can't trace God doesn't mean He's not working. (Romans 11:33) Truth is you must stand still and watch the Lord work on your behalf. And trust, HE IS WORKING!!!! (Exodus 14:13)

Remember, God is making things happen for YOU. Even when you don't see it, feel it or it's evident. He's still handling every single need.

Stay prayed up and encouraged, it is well!!!!!

"But you will not even need to fight. Take your positions; then stand still and watch the LORD's victory. He is with you," (2 Chronicles 20:17)

JANUARY 9

THE PATH

Life is going to come with options. One path can lead to silver and gold. And another can lead to diamonds and pearls. So, which do you pick?

Fact is you're going to have options. Just because a doorway opens - doesn't mean you have to walk through it.

Remember, it's one thing to feel that you are on the right path, but it's another to think that yours is the only path. (Paul Coelho)

"Seek His will in all you do, and He will show you which path to take." (Proverbs 3:6)

JANUARY 10

CHEERS

There are some folks in this world that no matter what you say or do. They still doubt and don't want you to succeed.

Truth is you're royalty and God's very own prized possession. (1 Peter 2:9) YOU WIN!!!! (1 Corinthians 15:57) No matter who doubts or says otherwise-they still can't take God's promises away from your life. (Jeremiah 29:11)

So, cheers to all the ones that are doubting you!!!!

"With God on our side we will win." (Psalm 108:13)

JANUARY 11

DO THE THING YOU THINK YOU CAN'T

At some point or another, we've all experienced fear. But the truth is God doesn't give us a spirit of fear. (2 Timothy 1:7) So, why are we afraid?

Today, do what you're most scared to do. God is attracted to your faith. (Hebrews 11:6) So, step out on faith and do what you think you can't!

Remember, you must do the thing you think you cannot do. (Eleanor Roosevelt)

"I can do all things through Him who strengthens me." (Philippians 4:13)

_____
_____
_____
_____
_____
_____
_____
_____
_____
_____
_____
_____
_____
_____
_____

JANUARY 12

RIGHT NOW ISN'T FOREVER

Your current situation might not be the best. But truth is it could be worse.

Yes! Where you are now is bad. It's sad and it's a dire situation. BUT GOD!!!!! We are pressed on every side by troubles, but we are not crushed. We are perplexed, but not driven to despair. (2 Corinthians 4:8) THIS TOO SHALL PASS!!!!!

Remember, where you are right now doesn't have to determine where you'll end up. (Barack Obama)

"We are hunted down, but never abandoned by God. We get knocked down, but we are not destroyed." (2 Corinthians 4:9)

_____
_____
_____
_____
_____
_____
_____
_____
_____
_____
_____
_____
_____

JANUARY 13

PRODIGIOUS STRENGTH

You've done all you can do. Yet it's still doesn't seem like it's enough. Sound familiar?

YES! You're tired, frustrated and it's seems God has forgotten about you. But truth is He's with you through all of the hurt and pain. (Deuteronomy 31:6)

Remember, there is prodigious strength in sorrow and despair. (Charles Dickens)

"Fear not, for I am with you; be not dismayed, for I am your God; I will strengthen you, I will help you, I will uphold you with my righteous right hand." (Isaiah 41:10)

JANUARY 14

DOUBT YOUR DOUBT

Doubting. Expressing a feeling of uncertainty or lack of conviction. How many has been there?

Truth is God doesn't give us a spirit of fear. (2 Timothy 1:7) But when our back is up against a wall, doubt and fear are what we encounter.

Today, when the enemy begins to creep in and you start to doubt, immediately, doubt your doubt!!!!

Remember, birds fly because they believe they can. All they have to do is open their wings and fly. You can too. (RVM)

"But let him ask in faith, with no doubting, for the one who doubts is like a wave of the sea that is driven and tossed by the wind." (James 1:6)

JANUARY 15

A DEAD FISH & A LIVE FISH

Things aren't going good. Tired of being sick and tired. Battle weary and frustrated. Sound familiar?

Who hasn't been there? In this life you're going to have good and bad days. But at the end of the day, life is still worth living!

Remember, a dead fish can float downstream, but it takes a live one to swim upstream. (W.C. Fields)

START SWIMMING!!!!!! The tide is turning!!!!

"When you go through deep waters, I will be with you. When you go through rivers of difficulty, you will not drown. When you walk through the fire of oppression, you will not be burned up; the flames will not consume you." (Isaiah 43:2)

JANUARY 16

BUILD YOUR MUSCLE UP

God doesn't give you a spirit of fear. (2 Timothy 1:7) Yet, you're still scared to step out on faith.

Truth is, without faith it is impossible to please God. (Hebrews 11:6) And you say you trust Him. So, know that He will not let you fall. (Psalm 121:3)

Remember, courage is what you need now. And like a muscle, it grows stronger every time we use it.

"Have I not commanded you? Be strong and courageous. Do not be frightened, and do not be dismayed, for the Lord your God is with you wherever you go." (Joshua 1:9)

JANUARY 17

LET THE AIR OUT OF YOUR BALLOON

I got 99 problems. How many can relate to that statement?

Yes! You might have problems. And your problem might be bigger than your neighbor's, or it could be smaller. At the end of the day, what you think is a problem might just be something you've blown out of proportion.

Remember, problems are like balloons. We let them unnecessarily blow up. (RVM)

"Do not be anxious about anything, but in everything by prayer and supplication with thanksgiving let your requests be made known to God." (Philippians 4:6)

JANUARY 18

IMPRESSING THE BIRD & HORSE

Unfortunately, life happens. The fairy tale that you dreamed of and even concocted can suddenly halt and change up. So, now what?

Now, you continue to press and move forward. (Philippians 3:14) YES! It's embarrassing, heartbreaking and even frustrating. But you're still standing. Who cares what others are saying and thinking. YOU have the Lord on your side. (Psalm 118:6)

Remember, one reason why birds and horses are not unhappy is because they are not trying to impress other birds and horses. (Dale Carnegie)

"So we speak, not to please man, but to please God who tests our hearts." (1 Thessalonians 2:4)

JANUARY 19

THE THOUGHT OF IT

Life and death are in the power of the tongue. (Proverbs 18:21) It's the same with your thoughts as well.

You can't sit and think of the bad and the negative of your situation. However, you can start to see and think of yourself healed, blessed and restored. (1 Peter 5:10)

Remember, don't let the thought of defeat itself defeat you.

"Do not conform to the pattern of this world but be transformed by the renewing of your mind. Then you will be able to test and approve what God's will is--His good, pleasing and perfect will." (Romans 12:2)

JANUARY 20

IT'S NOT TOO FAR

Wanting. Praying. Hoping and Desiring. Those are all things you do when you want something.

It doesn't matter if you're praying for a dream. A business idea, or weight loss. It's still a goal for you.

What you don't want to do is give up because it's seems impossible and untrainable. (Galatians 6:9)

Remember, it's not too far; it just seems like it is. (Yogi Berra)

"For nothing will be impossible with God."" (Luke 1:37)

JANUARY 21

STRONGER THAN YOU THINK

Giving up all hope. Shattered. Defeated. Discouraged and Crushed. That's how you feel in a broken place. BUT GOD!!!!!

Truth is folks are pressed and afflicted on every side by troubles, but not crushed. Perplexed, but not driven to despair. Persecuted, but not abandoned; struck down, but not destroyed. (2 Corinthians 4:8-9)

YOU ARE STRONGER THAN YOU THINK!!!

Remember, Life breaks us all but, in the end, we are stronger in the broken places. (Ernest Hemingway)

"Be strong and courageous; do not be frightened or dismayed, for the Lord your God is with you wherever you go."(Joshua 1:9)

_____

_____

_____

_____

_____

_____

_____

_____

_____

_____

JANUARY 22

PROGRESS IS IMPOSSIBLE WITHOUT CHANGE

Stubborn. Bullheaded. Headstrong. That's how folks act when they just don't want to change.

Fact is life is forever changing. And if you do things you've always done you'll keep getting the same results. So, it's time to do something different.

Remember, progress is impossible without change & those who cannot change their minds cannot change anything. (George Bernard Shaw)

"Therefore, if anyone is in Christ, he is a new creation. The old has passed away; behold, the new has come." (2 Corinthians 5:17)

JANUARY 23

STANDING TALL

Not everybody wants to see you win. Let's face it, there are those that are watching and waiting just for you to fail and fall. BUT GOD!!!

YES! You might be frustrated, agitated and ready to throw in the towel. But it's in those moments the most that you have to push and press harder to the mark.   (Philippians 3:14)

Remember, most people just want to see you fall, that's more reason to stand tall. (Emma Michelle)

(*Listen,* stay alert, stand tall in the faith, be courageous, and be strong. (1 Corinthians 16:13)

JANUARY 24

TIE A KNOT AND HOLD ON

Have you ever been at the end of your rope and just didn't know what to do? Letting go seems like the easy thing to do. BUT GOD!!!

See, we are hunted down, but never abandoned by God. We get knocked down, but we are not destroyed. (2 Corinthians 4:9)

Remember, when you're at the end of your rope, tie a knot and hold on. (Theodore Roosevelt)

"Let us hold tightly without wavering to the hope we affirm, for God can be trusted to keep His promise." (Hebrews 10:23)

JANUARY 25

YOU ARE WHAT YOU EAT

You are what you eat. I'm sure you've heard that phrase before. Meaning that if you eat good food you'll be healthier and fit.

The same goes with what you say about yourself. You are what you say you are. So, if you keep telling yourself...."You're amazing and you can do this." YOU CAN!!!

Remember, Muhammad Ali said he was the greatest even before he knew he was.

"I can do all things through Christ who gives me strength." (Philippians 4:13)

JANUARY 26

BY PERSEVERANCE YOU CAN

Frustrated. Tired. And now you just want to give up. Is that you? I get it. You're doing everything right and yet nothing is changing. Why wouldn't you want to give up?

However, you can't get weary in well doing. (Galatians 6:9) YES! You're tired. But those who trust in the Lord will find new strength. They will soar high on wings like eagles. They will run and not grow weary. They will walk and not faint. (Isaiah 40:31)

Remember, great works are performed, not by strength, but by perseverance. (Samuel Johnson)

"That's why I take pleasure in my weaknesses, and in the insults, hardships, persecutions, and troubles that I suffer for Christ. For

JANUARY 27

SERVE NOTICE TO THE ENEMY

Steal, kill and destroy. (John 10:10) That's what the enemy comes to do in your life. The question is are you prepared to handle the schemes and tricks that come with it?

Truth is you must always put on the full armor of God. So, that you can take your stand against the devil's schemes. (Ephesians 6:11)

Today, service notice to the enemy!!! No longer will you be scared, terrified or moved. And no longer will you fall victim to his lies, schemes and tricks. Fact is YOU WIN!!!! The devil is a lie!!!! (Psalm 1:3) (Psalm 108:13) (John 8:44)

"They will be like a tree planted by the water that sends out its roots by the stream. It does not fear when heat comes; its leaves are always green. It has no worries in a year of drought and never fails to bear fruit." (Jeremiah 17:8)

_____
_____
_____
_____
_____
_____
_____
_____
_____

JANUARY 28

GOSSIP & VERBAL DEFAMATION

Girl I got some juicy gossip for you. Boy I got to tell you something you won't believe. Sound familiar?

Whether you call it, "tea", gossip, juice or even the scoop. At the end of the day, it's still blathering and chit chattering. And it's something that you shouldn't be doing.

So, how would your life be different if...You walked away from gossip and verbal defamation? Let today be the day...You speak only the good you know of other people and encourage others to do the same. (Steve Maraboli)

"Without wood a fire goes out; without a gossip a quarrel dies down." (Proverbs 26:20)

_____
_____
_____
_____
_____
_____
_____
_____
_____
_____

JANUARY 29

GETTING BEAT DOWN

Kicked. Knocked down. Punched. Twists & Turns. That's what we call...LIFE.

And who hasn't experienced that type of a roller coaster ride? Almost as if you've gone ten rounds with the Heavyweight Boxing Champion of the World. BUT GOD!!!!

Remember, getting beat down might be the definition of your life... Getting back up is the definition of YOU!!!!!! (Cavan Holleran)

"If they fall, they will not stay down, because the LORD will help them up." (Psalm 37:24)

JANUARY 30

A BIRD, WORM & NEST

But I need _____ to move forward. I can't do it yet. Sound familiar?

Often our focus is on the "immediate" need. So, we don't even realize that God has already given us everything we need to go to the next level. (Philippians 4:19)

Remember, God gives every bird his worm, but He does not throw it into the nest. (P. D. James)

"And God is able to make all grace abound to you, so that in all things, at all times, having all that you need, you will abound in every good work." (2 Corinthians 9:8)

"If they fall, they will not stay down, because the LORD will help them up." (Psalm 37:24)

_____
_____
_____
_____
_____
_____
_____
_____
_____

JANUARY 31

FORGET ABOUT IT

How? What? When? And let's not forget, "The Waiting." Can you relate?

See, there comes a time in everyone's life when you have to be still and trust God. Yes! It looks bad and it's seems that He has forgotten you. But if the Lord can keep and feed the birds in the air; what makes you think YOU aren't as valuable as they? (Matthew 6:26)

Remember, never worry about the past, it brings tears. Don't think too much about the future, it brings fears. Live in the present moment with a smile it brings cheers!! (RVM)

"Therefore, do not worry about tomorrow, for tomorrow will worry about itself. Each day has enough trouble of its own." (Matthew 6:34)

FEBRUARY 1

EVERYTHING IS OUT OF CONTROL

Have you ever felt like everything is falling apart? It seems like your whole life is crumbling and out of control and there is nothing that you can do about it. Sound familiar?

Truth is there is something you can do. And that's turn everything over to the Lord. See, what you can do is one thing. But what God can do is another. (Psalms 55:22)

Remember, the reason your life is out of control is because you're afraid of giving control of your life to God. (Timothy Keller)

"I have considered my ways and have turned my steps to your statutes." (Psalm 119:59)

FEBRUARY 2

TAKE YOUR CUES FROM GOD

I don't know what I should do. Is this the right time to say something? After they go, then I'll make my move. Now, surely that's not you, is it?

Truth is you don't need to take any cues from anyone but the Lord. You're sitting and wondering what you should and shouldn't do, based on other people's moves. STOP!!!!

Remember, your cues come from God, not from folks.

"The LORD says, "I will guide you along the best pathway for your life. I will advise you and watch over you." (Psalm 32:8)

FEBRUARY 3

NO PRESSURE, NO DIAMONDS

Diamonds are formed under conditions of extreme temperature and pressure. Now how many of you agree that you're a diamond?

See, God has refined YOU. Though not as silver. But you've been tested in the furnace of affliction, trials and suffering. (Isaiah 48:10) And you're still standing.

Therefore, no pressure, no diamonds. (Thomas Carlyle)

"These trials will show that your faith is genuine. It is being tested as fire tests and purifies gold--though your faith is far more precious than mere gold. So, when your faith remains strong through many trials, it will bring you much praise and glory and honor on the day when Jesus Christ is revealed to the whole world." (1 Pete 1:7)

FEBRUARY 4

BUT I'M WORRIED ABOUT IT

Nonstop thinking. Worried. Stressing all over something that's out of your control. Can you relate?

Truth is, you have to pray. Give it to the Lord and let it go!!!!!! (Psalm 55:22) Getting yourself all worked up is doing nothing but adding additional stress you don't need.

So, today look around and enjoy all the beautiful things that surround you rather than yearn for things that are beyond your control that are keeping you miserable.

"Don't worry about anything; instead, pray about everything. Tell God what you need and thank Him for all he has done." (Philippians 4:6)

FEBRUARY 5

A LOSS & A GAIN

You win some and you lose some. That's life.

Truth is there are going to be some hurtful losses in your life that you aren't going to be able to control. Then there will be losses that are needed. But, God doesn't take away without replacing either. (Deuteronomy 30:3-13)

Remember, for everything you have missed, you have gained something else, and for everything you gain, you lose something else. (Ralph Waldo Emerson)

"The LORD gave, and the LORD has taken away; blessed be the name of the LORD."" (Job 1:21)

FEBRUARY 6

SO WHAT...THEY LEFT

They walked out on you. They cheated on you. Divorced you. Broke up with you. Left you. Now you're hurt. You feel like you can't go on. Depressed. Sobbing and stuck in bed. Sound familiar?

It doesn't matter if it was a relationship ending. A job that let you go. A friendship that came to a close. Truth is an end of a matter hurts.

Sometimes you just need to tell some folks: Boy bye or Girl bye! You're going to be just fine!!!

Remember, God never ties your destiny to those who left you but who remains or who is called to you. (Bishop Dale C. Bronner)

"They went out from us, but they did not really belong to us. For if they had belonged to us, they would have remained with us; but their going showed that none of them belonged to us." (1 John 2:19)

FEBRUARY 7

I'VE BEEN SUFFERING FOR TOO LONG

I'm tired. And I'm sick and tired of being sick and tired. Can you relate?

Let's face it. Life definitely has its trials. There will be good days and bad. But every day the Lord will be with you through them all. (Deuteronomy 31:6)

So, don't worry, stress or get weary. You're not in this alone!!! (Isaiah 41:10)

Remember, although the world is full of suffering, it is also full of the overcoming of it. (Helen Keller)

"And after you have suffered a little while, the God of all grace, who has called you to his eternal glory in Christ, will himself restore, confirm, strengthen, and establish you." (1 Peter 5:10)

_____
_____
_____
_____
_____
_____
_____
_____
_____

FEBRUARY 8

HAVE ENOUGH SENSE TO WALK AWAY

But you love them. It feels right. It's the best thing you've ever had. But _____. Has that been you? Always making excuses trying to justify why you should be somewhere you know God doesn't want you?

See, just as a dog returns to its vomit. So, are fools who keep repeating their foolishness. (Proverbs 26:11)

There comes a time that you have to know that God is trying to show YOU something. And before He takes you to the next level and elevates you. You need to reexamine some things that you're doing. (James 1:22)

Remember, a bad beginning makes a bad ending.

(Euripides)

"I listen carefully to what God the LORD is saying, for He speaks peace to His faithful people. But let them not return to their foolish ways." (Psalms 85:8)

FEBRUARY 9

IT'S IN PERFECT ORDER

Nothing is going right. You're tired. Frustrated. You're doing everything right and still...NOTHING. Sound familiar?

Everyone has been there before. Some folks are there now. But you can't get weary in well doing. Because you will reap your harvest if you don't give up! (Galatians 6:9)

Today, know that everything is in perfect order, whether you understand it or not. (Guy Finley)

So, "Trust in the LORD with all your heart, and do not lean on your own understanding." (Proverbs 3:5)

FEBRUARY 10

GOD HAS A BETTER ONE

Have you ever put a plan together that you knew was going to work? Every detail worked out to a "T". However, the plan suddenly got thwarted. Sound familiar?

See, there are many plans in our hearts. But it's the Lord's plans and His will in the end that's going to be established. (Proverbs 19:21)

So, you can concoct, plan and do what you want. But your plan might be good. But God's plan is better!!!!!

"Commit to the LORD whatever you do, and He will establish your plans." (Proverbs 16:3)

FEBRUARY 11

HOW ARE YOU BEHAVING?

Waiting. Who really likes to wait? We live in a society where we can get things instantly. However, the good ole 1984 Heinz ketchup campaign is so true. "Good things comes to those who wait."

I get it! You've prayed. You've fasted. You've been standing, yet still nothing. But you can't get weary while God is working. (Galatians 6:9) And YES! He is working. So, stand still and watch the deliverance of the Lord on your behalf. (Exodus 14:13)

Remember, patience is not simply the ability to wait – it's how we behave while we're waiting. (Joyce Meyer)

"Be still before the LORD and wait patiently for Him;" (Psalm 37:7)

FEBRUARY 12

CHECK YOURSELF

It's easy to blame others when they are blocking and standing in front of what you're wanting to do. But what do you do when the person stopping you is YOU?

Today, start checking your own self. So, instead of trying to figure out what others are doing and what and why things aren't happening. Take a look at what you're doing.

Remember, as long as a man stands in his own way, everything seems to be in his way. (Ralph Waldo Emerson)

"For each one should carry their own load." (Galatians 6:5)

FEBRUARY 13

A PROMISE KEEPER

Hopes. Dreams. Plans. Promises. All shattered. Now you're heartbroken, devastated and don't know what to do. Sound familiar?

Truth is what you do now is turn to the Lord. YES! It didn't work out. But what you wanted God didn't want for you. So, it had to end. (Psalm 121:7)

Remember, God knew you before you were born. He already knows how this will end. And it is well!!!!!!!! (Jeremiah 1:5) & (Jeremiah 29:11)

"God is not human, that he should lie, not a human being, that he should change his mind. Does he speak and then not act? Does he promise and not fulfill?" (Numbers 23:19)

FEBRUARY 14

YES! IT'S VALENTINE'S DAY

Today is Valentine's Day. Known as the celebration of romance and romantic love all around the world. So, folks will be going to dinner. Sending roses. Eating chocolates and professing their love to one another. All happy, filled with love and joy.

However, everyone isn't so joyous on this day. There are a lot of other folks that hate today and walk around sad and depressed.

YES! The Divorce. Breakup. Loss. All have been hard to deal with. But that doesn't mean that you're still not loved. At the end of the day, you must know that folks will come and go. But God will never leave nor forsake you. (Isaiah 41:10)

Remember, whether you're with someone special today or not. You're loved by God!

Happy Valentine's Day!!!!

"Because you are precious in my sight and honored, and I love you," (Isaiah 43:4)

_____
_____
_____
_____
_____
_____
_____
_____

FEBRUARY 15

STOP TOUCHING IT

Have you ever scraped your knee or had an open sore on your body? And, for whatever reason, you just had to keep picking at it?

See, that's how folks do with the past and situations in life. God wants you to leave it alone and move on. (Isaiah 43:19) But you just keep picking and picking and picking at it. STOP!!!

Remember, to heal a wound stop touching it!

"He heals the broken-hearted and binds up their wounds." (Psalm 147:3)

FEBRUARY 16

IT'S TOO EXPENSIVE

Have you ever seen an expensive outfit, shoes or handbag that you really liked and wanted. But it just cost way too much. However, you got it and you knew you shouldn't have because you had other obligations. And then you get stressed out about it. Sound familiar?

Folks, there are some things that just shouldn't cost your peace. Whether that's a Relationship. Job. Clothes or Environment. At what cost are you willing to pay?

Remember, if something costs your peace, it's too expensive! (Bishop Dale C. Bronner)

"Now may the Lord of peace himself give you his peace at all times and in every situation. The Lord be with you all." (2 Thessalonians 3:16)

FEBRUARY 17

GOD'S IN CHARGE

I have to do this. I need to call to see if this can be done. I hope they can help. Sound familiar?

See, when crisis hits often we tend to call on everybody but the name of the Lord. (Romans 10:13) Truth is God is always in charge the entire time.

God will never leave nor forsake you. (Deuteronomy 31:6) You might feel like the storm caught you off guard. But nothing happened that has struck God by surprise. (Jeremiah 29:11)

At the end of the day, Beloved, there is nothing to fear. God is in charge!!!!!!!

It is well!!!!!!

"Don't be afraid! I am the First and the Last." (Revelation 1:17)

FEBRUARY 18

CHANGE YOUR WORLD WITH YOUR WORDS

Life is unfair. Nothing is going right. Problems from the North, South, East and West. Sound familiar?

So, are you going to wallow in your trials and tribulations? Or are you going to fight and stand in faith?

Truth is, you must fight the good fight of faith. (1 Timothy 6:12) Speak and declare as if everything you need is already done. (Mark 11:22-24)

Remember, God isn't attracted to your problems, but He is attracted to your praise and your reaction to your problems.

IT IS WELL!!!!!

"So shall my word be that goes out from my mouth; it shall not return to me empty, but it shall accomplish that which I purpose, and shall succeed in the thing for which I sent it." (Isaiah 55:11)

FEBRUARY 19

FORGIVE YOUR ENEMY

How many of you would say you have or had an enemy in your life? You might not even be aware that you had one. For whatever reason it could be because of the anointing on your life that causes them not to like you.

At the end of the day - you can go as low as them and be malicious and wicked. Or you could just rise above. Forgive, forget and move on. (Ephesians 4:32)

Remember, always forgive your enemies; it's not about them. It's about you!

"But I say to you, 'Love your enemies and pray for those who persecute you'" (Matthew 5:44)

FEBRUARY 20

YOU SIN TOO

She had a baby out of wedlock and you talked about her. But you had a baby by a married man and hid it. He hides the fact that he is an alcoholic. But he talks about his neighbor that's addicted to porn. But that's not you...Is it?

Folks, sin is sin!!!! Just because your sin is different than your neighbor. That doesn't make you any better than them. At the end of the day- it is still SIN!!!!!!! (John 8:7)

Remember, you cannot judge people because they sin differently than you. (Erykah Badu)

""Judge not, and you will not be judged; condemn not, and you will not be condemned; forgive, and you will be forgiven;" (Luke 6:37)

FEBRUARY 21

GOOD RIDDANCE

It's hard to say goodbye, sometimes. However, in some cases, it's necessary.

Yes! Things aren't working out quite how you planned. But guess what? Stop leaning and depending on your way and trust in the Lord. He is going to direct your path. BUT, it will happen in His time and not yours. (Proverbs 3:5-6)

Remember, sometimes life is going to cause doors to close for you because it's time to move forward. It's a good thing. So, say good riddance and receive the new blessing the Lord is bringing forth!

"A person's steps are directed by the LORD, and the LORD delights in his way." (Psalm 37:23)

FEBRUARY 22

DRINKING TEARS FOR WATER

Hurt. Can't believe this. Devastated. Broken. Have you ever been there before? Are you there now?

I get it. But it's okay! See, this probably feels like this is the worst time of your life and nobody can relate to how you feel. Folks wouldn't believe that you're drinking tears for water. But God is with you through all of this. (Deuteronomy 31:8)

At the end of the day, no matter how bad it looks. God has the final say through every battle, every struggle and every storm.

"We may make our plans, but God has the last word." (Proverbs 16:1)

_____
_____
_____
_____
_____
_____
_____
_____
_____
_____
_____
_____
_____
_____

FEBRUARY 23

CHANGE THE CHORD IN YOUR VOICE

I want a change. I need something new. I want. I want. I want. Sound familiar?

Often, folks sit and talk about what they want to change in their life. But they're sitting there mute.

Truth is maybe you're not seeing anything because you're not saying anything. (Proverbs 18:21)

Remember, if you want to change your environment and your world. Change the chord in your voice. (Pastor Jamal Bryant)

God says if I hear something you'll see something!!!!!!

"And this is the confidence that we have toward Him, that if we ask anything according to His will He hears us. And if we know that He hears us in whatever we ask, we know that we have the requests that we have asked of Him. (1 John 5:14-15)

FEBRUARY 24

THE BEST SPEECH YOU WILL EVER REGRET

Mad. Angry. Furious. Enraged. Can you relate to those feelings? See, the worst thing you can do is to act on those feelings when you're in that state.

I get it. You're heated, you want to release those emotions. But you can't.

Always remember this: speak when you are angry, and you will make the best speech you will ever regret. (Ambrose Bierce)

"Understand this, my dear brothers and sisters: You must all be quick to listen, slow to speak, and slow to get angry." (James 1:19)

FEBRUARY 25

FREE YOUR MIND

I believe God. I trust God. I'm going to step out on faith. Oh Lord what am I going to do? I'm scared. I don't know what's going to happen now. Sound familiar?

See, two things can't operate your mind at the same time. (Matthew 6:24) You're reading your Word. But then the enemy gets in your head and you start to believe his lies. Folks the devil is a lie!!!!! There is NO truth in him!!!! (John 8:44)

Fact is, God is GOD!!!! (Deuteronomy 10:17) He is not like man that he shall lie. If He says it, it will come to pass. (Numbers 23:19)

So, stop worrying because what you've stepped out on isn't happening right now. Or what you've sown hasn't risen yet. Stand and leave it alone and let God work!!!! (Exodus 14:13)

"By His power, God raised the Lord from the dead, and He will raise us also." (1 Corinthians 6:14)

FEBRUARY 26

POISON

When most people think of poison they think of harmful venom or a substance that can cause illness or death. So, why would you not want to stay away from it?

Unfortunately, poison has a way of being around you, even when you think they aren't poisonous. But what the enemy means for evil, God will use for your good. (Genesis 50:20)

Remember, there are poisons that blind you and poisons that open your eyes. (August Strindberg)

"They will be able to handle snakes with safety, and if they drink anything poisonous, it won't hurt them. They will be able to place their hands on the sick, and they will be healed."" (Mark 16:18)

FEBRUARY 27

KEEP RIDING YOUR BICYCLE

As a child can you remember what it is was like learning to ride your first bicycle? More than likely, you fell a couple of times. But you got back on your bike. Right?

In life, you're going to have some rough roads ahead. There are going to be some hard and stressful trials that you're going to be faced with. And as much as you want to give up. You must keep pressing forward. (Philippians 3:14)

Remember, life is like riding a bicycle. To keep your balance, you must keep moving. (Albert Einstein)

"So, let's not get tired of doing what is good. At just the right time, we will reap a harvest of blessing if we don't give up." (Galatians 6:9)

_____

_____

_____

_____

_____

_____

_____

_____

_____

_____

FEBRUARY 28

YOU HAVE TO FACE IT

There are some things in life that you just don't want to face or deal with. I get it! So, are you going to just hold everything in and not deal with them? NO!

As hard as it is to face. You must deal with ALL challenges head on and know that you are not alone. (Deuteronomy 31:6)

Remember, not everything that is faced can be changed, but nothing can be changed until it is faced. (James Baldwin)

"Count it all joy, my brothers, when you meet trials of various kinds, for you know that the testing of your faith produces steadfastness. And let steadfastness have its full effect, that you may be perfect and complete, lacking in nothing." (James 1:2-4)

MARCH 1

IT'S GOING TO COST YOU

Expense is a cost required for something. And that is exactly what happens when you keep holding on to your past.

At what point are you going to keep reliving the pain and the hurt? See, it's time to release. Let Go. And let God!!!! (Isaiah 41:10)

Remember, when you hold on to your history you do it at the expense of your destiny.

(Bishop T.D. Jakes)

"Remember not the former things, nor consider the things of old. Behold, I am doing a new thing; now it springs forth, do you not perceive it? I will make a way in the wilderness and rivers in the desert." (Isaiah 43:18-19)

_____
_____
_____
_____
_____
_____
_____
_____
_____
_____
_____
_____

MARCH 2

HOW ARE YOU GOING TO REACT?

Mean and surly. You know folks like that? It can seem like no matter how nice you are they still can be grouchy and evil.

So, are you going to get on their level and do like them? NO! Because you must love and be kind to those even when they are nasty in their ways. (Luke 6:28)

Truth is you don't know what is going on with them and why they are acting the way they are. But kind words go far.

Remember, how people treat you is their karma; how you react is yours. (Wayne Dyer)

"The point is this: whoever sows sparingly will also reap sparingly, and whoever sows bountifully will also reap bountifully. Each one must give as he has decided in his heart, not reluctantly or under compulsion, for God loves a cheerful giver. And God is able to make all grace abound to you, so that having all sufficiency in all things at all times, you may abound in every good work." (2 Corinthians 9:6-8)

_____

_____

_____

_____

_____

_____

_____

_____

MARCH 3

BE CALM WHILE YOU WAIT

Patience is a virtue. How many of you have heard that before? Fact is it's good to have patience. But easier said than done.

However, God doesn't give us a spirit of fear, but of power, love and self-control. (2 Timothy 1:7) So, you can endure the wait.

Remember, patience is not the ability to wait. Patience is to be calm no matter what happens, constantly take action to turn it to positive growth opportunities, and have faith to believe that it will all work out in the end while you are waiting. (Roy T. Bennett)

"But if we hope for what we do not see, we wait for it with patience." (Romans 8:25)

MARCH 4

NO ENEMY WITHIN

When you get to a point when you're not self-judging your own self. Or dealing with an inner critic. Nobody else can hurt you. (Exodus 14:14)

Now, that doesn't mean you don't hurt, feel or get disappointed by what others say or do. NO! You just let the Lord handle them and be still!!!

Remember, when there is no enemy within, the enemies outside cannot hurt you. (Winston Churchill)

"'Do not fear them, for the LORD your God is the one fighting for

MARCH 5

NOW WHAT

You just lost your job. The doctor just gave you a bad report. Your spouse just left you. You don't have any money left in the bank. Now what?

Now...You call on the name of JESUS!!!! (Acts 4:12)

At the end of the day no matter how bad it looks. Know that God is a Healer. Protector. Redeemer. Almighty. Eternal. Alpha & Omega. He is ALL you need!!!! (2 Thessalonians 1:2-12)

Remember, you never know God is all you need until God is all you have. (Rick Warren)

ALL IS WELL!!!!!!

"And we know that God causes everything to work together for the good of those who love God and are called according to His purpose

_____
_____
_____
_____
_____
_____
_____
_____
_____
_____

MARCH 6

YOU'RE DOING THE WRONG THING

It's easy to cry, whine and complain about what you're going through. I get it! But what are you really fixing by doing that? NOTHING!!!

You're going to have to quit calling any and everybody about your problem and what you're going through. Instead, call on the name of the Lord. He is the ONLY ONE that you need. (Psalm 16:5-11)

Remember, if you prayed as much as you complain and quarrel, you'd have a lot less to argue about and much more peace of mind. (Rick Warren)

"Do not be anxious about anything, but in everything by prayer and supplication with thanksgiving let your requests be made known to God. And the peace of God, which surpasses all understanding, will guard your hearts and your minds in Christ Jesus." (Philippians 4:6-7)

MARCH 7

WHEN ARE YOU GOING TO BEGIN

The restaurant. The book. The shop. The album. The idea. You have a dream but you're not doing anything with it. Sound familiar?

See, God has given you a dream and a vision inside of you. So, what are you waiting for?

Remember, you will never win if you never begin. (Helen Rowland)

"Now finish the work, so that your eager willingness to do it may be matched by your completion of it, according to your means." (2 Corinthians 8:11)

MARCH 8

STRESSFUL THINKING

I'm so stressed out. Sound familiar? It seems like every other day you're overwhelmed. But are you really?

YES! To look at the situation it seems bleak. But we walk by faith and not by sight. (2 Corinthians 5:7) And everything that you're worried and stressed about God has already worked out. (Exodus 14:13)

Remember, the truth is that there is no actual stress or anxiety in the world; it's your thoughts that create these false beliefs. You can't package stress, touch it, or see it. There are only people engaged in stressful thinking. (Wayne Dyer)

"Peace I leave with you; my peace I give to you. Not as the world gives do I give to you. Let not your hearts be troubled, neither let them be afraid." (John 14:27)

_____
_____
_____
_____
_____
_____
_____
_____
_____
_____

MARCH 9

WHEN TROUBLE COMES BACK FOR AN ENCORE

Have you ever looked back in the rearview mirror of your life and just thanked God? I'm talking about really reflecting about the dangerous and treacherous situations you've escaped, and you know it was nothing BUT the Lord that kept and protected YOU. (Numbers 6:24)

Truth is the years have come and gone. The seasons have changed. But praise be to God that you aren't who you used to be. (Isaiah 43:18)

Remember, you don't know how much you've grown- until trouble comes back for an encore. (Bishop T.D. Jakes)

"Therefore, if anyone is in Christ, the new creation has come: The old has gone, the new is here! (2 Corinthians 5:17)

MARCH 10

STOP WATERING CONCRETE

When you water flowers or a garden what happens? The seed grows. Now, have you ever thought about the things in your life that you shouldn't be watering?

It's time to stop watering the "dead" in your life. Dead relationships. Dead issues. Dead people. You can't keep feeding what no longer serves you good. So, stop watering things that were never meant to grow in your life.

Remember, water what works, what's good, what's right. Stop playing around with those dead bones and stuff you can't fix, it's over...leave it alone! You're coming into a season of greatness. If you water what's alive and divine, you will see harvest like you've never seen before. No matter how much you water concrete, you can't grow a garden. (Bishop T.D. Jakes)

""It was planted in good soil beside abundant waters, that it might yield branches and bear fruit and become a splendid vine."" (Ezekiel 17:8)

MARCH 11

ZIP IT!!!

You say something. Then they say something. Before you know it you both are mumbling things under your breath trying to have the final word. Can you relate?

Having the last word in argument can cause the conflict to go on and on. There comes a time that you must zip it!!!!

Remember, silence is one of the hardest arguments to refute. (Josh Billings)

"Again, I say, don't get involved in foolish, ignorant arguments that only start fights." (2 Timothy 2:23)

"Even a fool who keeps silent is considered wise; when he closes his lips, he is deemed intelligent." (Proverbs 17:28)

MARCH 12

THIS WILL BE ONE DAY AS IF IT NEVER WAS

Have you ever wished that what you were going through would just cease and desist? I mean it's the worst time of your life. I get it. But what doesn't kill you only makes you stronger.

Fact is you have to endure through the trials, heartache and struggle. More than that, we rejoice in our sufferings, knowing that suffering produces endurance, and endurance produces character, and character produces hope. (Romans 5:3-4)

Remember, strength of character isn't always about how much you can handle before you break, it's also about how much you can handle after you've broken. (Robert Tew)

"But he said to me, "My grace is sufficient for you, for my power is made perfect in weakness." Therefore, I will boast all the more gladly of my weaknesses, so that the power of Christ may rest upon me. For the sake of Christ, then, I am content with weaknesses, insults, hardships, persecutions, and calamities. For when I am weak, then I am strong." (2 Corinthians 12:9-10)

_____

_____

_____

_____

_____

_____

_____

_____

MARCH 13

WHAT HAPPENED TO YOU?

When folks start to think about their past, some get angry. Others cry. A few get sad. But at the end of the day, it's the past. It's done with and a new day has come. (Isaiah 43:19)

So, does that mean you should forget? NO! But it does mean that you can't let your past keep defining what you do in moving forward. It's time to forgive, forget and let it go. (Matthew 6:14-15)

Remember, it doesn't matter what happens to you. What matters is what you're going to do about it. Are you going to complain and shrink or are you going to step into your greatness? (Robert Tew)

"Therefore, if anyone is in Christ, he is a new creation. The old has passed away. Behold, the new has come!" (2 Corinthians 5:17)

MARCH 14

I DON'T MEAN NO HARM.... BUT

Have you ever heard someone say, "I don't mean no harm? BUT... then, they completely mean harm in what they say next?

Truth is there shouldn't be any foul and corrupting talk that comes out of your mouth. However, you should be building up one another instead of trying to judge and tear down. (Ephesians 4:29)

Remember, there's a story behind every person. There's a reason why they're the way they are. Think about that before you judge anyone. (Ziad K. Abdelnour)

At the end of the day, you labeling someone doesn't define who they are. It says who you are!!!!

Do not judge, or you too will be judged. For in the same way you judge others, you will be judged, and with the measure you use, it will be measured to you." (Matthew 7:1-2)

MARCH 15

STRONG ENOUGH TO STAND UP AGAIN

You've been knocked, pushed and, in some cases, kicked to the ground. So, what do you do? You get back up!!

If someone knocks you down, that's on them. But if you're still down three days later... that's on YOU!!! (Al Sharpton) You must make up your mind, "This is not how my story is going to end."

Remember, be strong enough to stand up again, even after haters make you drop to your knees. (Bishop T.D. Jakes)

"For though the righteous fall seven times, they rise again," (Proverbs 24:16)

"We are hunted down, but never abandoned by God. We get knocked down, but we are not destroyed." (2Corinthians 4:9)

MARCH 16

WHAT'S THE STORY YOU'RE TELLING YOURSELF?

I don't have the time to do this. My condition keeps me from moving forward. Sound familiar?

Truth is when you keep telling yourself you can't and won't. That's exactly what will happen…. NOTHING!

Remember, the story you tell yourself is often a shelter that shades you from the truth of what it takes to change. (Bishop T.D. Jakes)

"Say to the righteous that it will go well with them. For they will eat the fruit of their actions." (Isaiah 3:10)

MARCH 17

USE THE BRICKS THROWN AT YOU

Do you ever feel like there are bricks thrown at you constantly? I get it! You want to throw some back.

However, God says it is mine to avenge and repay. (Deuteronomy 32:35) YES! They threw some bricks. Now it's time for you to use what was thrown at you.

Remember, build your Kingdom with the same bricks thrown at you. (Derrick Fuller)

"May the LORD judge between you and me. And may the LORD avenge the wrongs you have done to me, but my hand will not touch you." (1 Samuel 24:12)

_____
_____
_____
_____
_____
_____
_____
_____
_____
_____
_____
_____
_____

MARCH 18

YOUR MIRROR IS BEING POLISHED

Irritated, frustrated and tired of being sick and tired. Sound familiar? So, what do you do?

See, it's easy to get infuriated and rattled by the storms that blow your way. But blessed is the one who perseveres under trial and rejoices in suffering. Because you will receive the crown of life that God has promised to those who love Him. (Romans 5:3) (James 1:12)

Remember, if you are irritated by every rub, how will your mirror be polished? (Rumi)

"These trials will show that your faith is genuine. It is being tested as fire tests and purifies gold—though your faith is far more precious than mere gold. So, when your faith remains strong through many trials, it will bring you much praise and glory and honor on the day when Jesus Christ is revealed to the whole world." (1 Peter 1:7)

MARCH 19

COMPLAINING OF A HEADACHE

Do you know people who are constantly complaining? I mean every time you turn around, they're complaining about something. But that's not YOU, is it?

You see, there is no need to complain if you are the problem. It's one thing if the issue that is happening to you can't be controlled. But what happens when YOU are the problem?

Remember, don't be the one who spends the day complaining of a headache, and in the night drinking the wine that gives it. (Johann Wolfgang Von Goethe)

"Neither are you to grumble, as some of them grumbled, and perished by the Destroyer." (1 Corinthians 10:10)

MARCH 20

BUT YOU GAVE THEM ACCESS

You pray, stand, fast and ask God to remove what's been hurting you. But you keep allowing whatever it is that's hurting you back in your life.

There comes a time in your life that you must realize that everything that's happening to you isn't the enemy. It's YOU! Because you're allowing it.

Remember, you cannot rebuke a devil that you continuously grant access to your life. (Bishop T.D. Jakes)

"Put on all of God's armor so that you will be able to stand firm against all strategies of the devil." (Ephesians 6:11)

MARCH 21

YOU'VE SURVIVED A LOT

Truth is you don't look like what you've been through. That's a shout que for everyone!!

Your life has had its ups and downs but, through it all, you're still standing. So, never doubt the storms that are sweeping your way. Why? Because you've been through worst.

Remember, trust yourself. You've survived a lot, and you'll survive whatever is coming. (Robert Tew)

"For I am the LORD your God who takes hold of your right hand and says to you, 'Do not fear; I will help you.'" (Isaiah 41:13)

MARCH 22

YOU'RE ASKING THE WRONG QUESTIONS

Why are you doing this to me? What is wrong with you? Why is this happening? Sound familiar?

Have you ever found yourself constantly asking the questions of why, what and how? At some point, you're going to have to stop asking all the questions and decide to walk away from the foolishness. Why? Because you love yourself more.

Remember, don't ask why people keep hurting you. Ask yourself why are you allowing it to happen? (Robert Tew)

"As a dog returns to its vomit, so also a fool repeats his foolishness." (Proverbs 26:11)

MARCH 23

THE MISTAKE YOU MADE

But only if I would have done that. What if I did it like this though? How many of you beat yourself up about a mistake that you made? The woulda, coulda and shouldas can drive you crazy.

Fact is it's over with. It happened. So, let it go!! Now, you're not insane. And insanity is doing the same thing over and over again expecting different results. (Albert Einstein)

You must learn from the mistake and move on!!!! (1 John 1:9)

Remember, don't cling to a mistake just because you spent a lot of time making it. (Aubrey de Grey)

"Brothers and sisters, I do not consider myself yet to have taken hold of it. But one thing I do: Forgetting what is behind and straining toward what is ahead," (Philippians 3:13)

MARCH 24

THE LEAVES AREN'T WORRIED

The deaths. They left. You lost. Things were taken from you. You keep asking God why, but more losses keep occurring. Sound familiar?

I get it. I too can relate. But do you jump out of an airplane due to turbulence? NO! You sit there and put your trust in the pilot to land you safely to your destination.

So, sit and wait patiently on the Lord to deliver you from your storm and turbulence in your life.   YES! The losses are painful. But God is a God of restoration and healing. (Jeremiah 30:17)

This too shall pass!!!!!!!

Remember, all the trees are losing their leaves, and not one of them is worried. (Donald Miller)

"Say to those who have an anxious heart, "Be strong; fear not! Behold, your God will come with vengeance, with the recompense of God. He will come and save you." (Isaiah 35:4)

MARCH 25

YOU MADE IT...NOW LIE IN IT!!!

Have you ever heard the expression "You've made your bed, now lie in it"? It's mostly a response to people who have been complaining about problems they brought on themselves. They made some bad decisions, and now they're paying the consequences.

The same goes for your relationship with God. For whatever one sows, they will also reap. (Galatians 6:7)

Remember nobody ever did, or ever will, escape the consequences of his choices. (Alfred A. Monapert)

So, watch what you're doing. Make good decisions so that this line doesn't describe you.

"He has dug a pit and hollowed it out and has fallen into the hole which he made." (Psalm 7:15)

_____

_____

_____

_____

_____

_____

_____

_____

_____

_____

MARCH 26

"F" -- YOU FAILED!

Have you ever failed at something, and it just plain devastated you? I get it! No one wants to fail, but you must ask yourself "Did I really fail?"

Often, what we think is a loss and failure in life is God actually setting us up for our next blessings. If God allowed it, that means that He has something better in store.

So, don't trip, cry and be disappointed over the loss. Better is around the corner.

Remember, forget about the consequences of failure. It's only a temporary change in direction to set you straight for your next success. (Denis Waitley)

"But I tell you the truth, it is for your benefit that I am going away. Unless I go away, the Advocate will not come to you; but if I go, I will send Him to you." (John 16:7)

_____
_____
_____
_____
_____
_____
_____
_____
_____

MARCH 27

THIS IS NOT WHAT I WANTED

Have you ever been so discouraged and upset because you wanted something to go as planned? But before you knew it, everything was falling apart. Sound familiar?

The easy thing to do is get upset, irritated and keep asking God, Why? However, instead of acting a fool because it didn't go the way YOU wanted. Rejoice and praise that God just protected you from what you couldn't see. (James 1:2-8)

Fact is you never know what harm is ahead of you and what God is keeping you from. (Psalm 121:7) He knows how the story ends. And just because you want it to go your way…doesn't mean it's the best way. (Jeremiah 1:5)

God ALWAYS knows best! (Isaiah 46:10)

Remember, sometimes when things go wrong it's because they would have turned out worse, if they had gone right. (Mark Amend)

""Behold, I am with you and will keep you wherever you go," (Genesis 28:15)

_____
_____
_____
_____
_____
_____
_____

MARCH 28

THE TRUTH OR A LIE

It's not true. That's a lie. Now, you're all upset and bent out of shape because you know what folks are saying is a lie.

Truth be told that is the story of a lot of folk's lives. However, you don't have to keep defending the truth. The truth will always be TRUE no matter how much a person lies!!!

Remember, TRUTH, doesn't need you to believe it. It is self-confident. It lives whether you believe or not. LIES, however, need you to believe them or they die. They insecurely beg, plead and try to convince you to believe. (Bruce Van Horn)

"And you will know the truth, and the truth will set you free." (John 8:32)

MARCH 29

STOP RAISING THE DEAD!!!!

They left, and yet you keep calling, begging and banging on the door. You plead, trying to get them to stay or come back. Why? Maya Angelou said it best, "When people show you who they are, believe them."

Fact is they showed you they meant it for evil, yet you keep on taking it. YOU deserve better. Let them GO!!!! (Genesis 50:20)

Remember, your destiny is never tied to those who left!!!!! (Bishop T.D. Jakes)

"They went out from us, but they did not really belong to us. For if they had belonged to us, they would have remained with us; but their going showed that none of them belonged to us." (1 John 2:19)

_____
_____
_____
_____
_____
_____
_____
_____
_____
_____
_____

MARCH 30

THE TRIAL OF MY LIFE

Shocked. Disbelief. Speechless. Dismayed. These are all feelings you get when life can take you by surprise. Have you been surprised by trials lately?

Well don't be surprised at the fiery trials you're going through, as if something strange is happening to you. Realize that everything that is taking place will be revealed so you can see God's glory in the end on your behalf. YOU got this!!!!!! (1 Peter 4:12-13)

Remember, a gem cannot be polished without friction, nor a man perfected without trials. (Lucius Annaeus Seneca)

"These trials will show that your faith is genuine. It is being tested as fire tests and purifies gold--though your faith is far more precious than mere gold. So, when your faith remains strong through many trials, it will bring you much praise and glory and honor on the day when Jesus Christ is revealed to the whole world." (1 Peter 1:7)

MARCH 31

STUCK IN THE CORNER

They said they were going to help you. Yet, they are nowhere to be found. Now, surely you haven't experienced that type of betrayal.

Just because "they" let you down doesn't mean that you stop. At the end of the day it's your vision and dream. You wrote it down... now you must run with it. (Habakkuk 2:2)

Remember, you can't stay in your corner of the Forest waiting for others to come to you. You have to go to them sometimes. (A.A. Milne)

"For if anyone is a hearer of the word and not a doer, he is like a man who looks intently at his natural face in a mirror. For he looks at himself and goes away and at once forgets what he was like. But the one who looks into the perfect law, the law of liberty, and perseveres, being no hearer who forgets but a doer who acts, he will be blessed in

_____
_____
_____
_____
_____
_____
_____
_____

APRIL 1

AND THIS IS HOW YOU TREAT ME

Have you ever poured your heart and soul into something or someone? And with a snap of a finger, they forget about you or what you've done for them.

I get it. It's wrong. However, when the wicked are mean and malicious, you still can't get down to their level. You must rise above what they're doing to you. No matter how bad you want to express yourself. (Proverbs 24:29)

Remember, respond intelligently even to unintelligent treatment. (Lao Tzu)

"For God is not unjust. He will not forget how hard you have worked for Him and how you have shown your love to Him by caring for

_____
_____
_____
_____
_____
_____
_____
_____
_____
_____

APRIL 2

TIME & KARMA

The same person you see going up. You will see going back down. I'm sure you heard that saying before.

Fact is it's true. Folks can get a big head and forget their humbling beginnings. But God can't be mocked; you will reap what you sow. (Galatians 6:9)

Remember this, when a bird is alive it eats ants. But when the bird passes away and dies, it's ants that then eat on the flesh of the dead bird. And one tree can make up a million matchsticks. However, it only takes one matchstick to burn up a million trees in a forest.

My point is this.... Circumstances can change at a drop of a dime and at any given time. So, YOU might be on top today. But God can shift your situation with a snap of a finger. Power is one thing. But time is more powerful than YOU!!!!!!

STAY WOKE!!!!!!!!!!!!!!!

Why, you do not even know what will happen tomorrow. What is your life? You are a mist that appears for a little while and then vanishes. (James 4:14)

_____
_____
_____
_____
_____
_____

APRIL 3

WHO CARES? I'M ANGRY

Crying, yelling and raging -- all at the same time. Has that been you?

See, it's a dangerous situation when things get so out of control and you can't handle your emotions. Truth is you must not let your spirit rush to become angry so quickly. Think before you act. (Ecclesiastes 7:9)

Remember, be patient when you are frustrated. Be silent when you are angry. Be brave when you are confronted with challenges. (Dr T.P.Chia)

"My dear brothers and sisters, take note of this: Everyone should be quick to listen, slow to speak and slow to become angry," (James 1:19)

_____
_____
_____
_____
_____
_____
_____
_____
_____
_____

APRIL 4

YOU FAILED, NOW WHAT?

Let's face it, nobody wants to fail. Especially if they are stepping out on faith and trying something only for it to flop.

However, the righteous may fall but they will rise again. (Proverbs 24:16). YES! It didn't work out the way you thought. So, does that mean you give up and walk away? NO! But it does mean you must continue to fight the good fight of faith. (1 Timothy 6:12) Because when you're weak, you are really strong!!!!! (2 Corinthians 12:9-10)

Remember, keep on beginning and failing. Each time you fail, start all over again, and you will grow stronger until you have accomplished a purpose - not the one you began with perhaps, but one you'll be glad to remember. (Anne Sullivan)

"My flesh and my heart may fail, but God is the strength of my heart and my portion forever." (Psalm 73:26)

APRIL 5

A RUINED FUTURE

When some folks think about the past it might make them cry. The pain and hurt is just too much to bear. But the fact remains the past happened and it's over with.

So, there comes a time in your life that you must move on. Now does that mean you forget? NO! But you don't let worry, fear and anxiety stop you from pressing forward to what God has in store for you next.

Remember, you can't change the past, but you can ruin the present by worrying about the future.

(Isak Dinesen)

"Brothers and sisters, I do not consider myself yet to have taken hold of it. But one thing I do: Forgetting what is behind and straining toward what is ahead," (Philippians 3:13)

APRIL 6

BUT I WANT TO GO NOW

I'm sick and tired of being here. I'm ready to GO!!!! Can you relate? You have to think of a newborn baby girl that's in her mother's womb that is ready to come out. But the baby is only 6 months old. So, technically she still needs time in the womb to develop. Fact is, it's not time yet.

And just like you're ready to make a move and hop, skip and jump. It's not your time yet either. What you want now doesn't mean that God wants it for you right now. (Habakkuk 2:3)

Remember, you can't go where you're not called, and if you do go, you can't stay. (Bishop Dale C. Bronner)

Wait for the Lord; be strong and let your heart take courage; wait for the Lord! (Psalm 27:14)

"Trust in the Lord with all your heart, and do not lean on your own understanding. In all your ways acknowledge Him, and He will make straight your paths." (Proverbs 3:5-6)

_____
_____
_____
_____
_____
_____
_____
_____

APRIL 7

STOP LETTING TRIFLES DISTURB YOUR TRANQUILITY

Stressed. Worried. Frightened. However, you know God doesn't give us a spirit of fear. (2 Timothy 1:7) But you're terrified and uneasy by the things that are taking place. Now, that's not you, is it?

1 Peter 5:8 tells us to be sober-minded and watchful. Because our adversary, the devil, prowls around like a roaring lion, seeking someone to devour. The enemy wants us afraid. But the devil is a lie!!!!! (John 8:44)

Remember, do not let trifles disturb your tranquility of mind. The little pin-pricks of daily life when dwelt upon and magnified, may do great damage, but if ignored or dismissed from thought, will disappear from inanition. (Grenville Kleiser)

"Submit yourselves therefore to God. Resist the devil, and he will flee from you." (James 4:7)

APRIL 8

FAKES & FRAUDS ARE UNQUALIFIED

Just get out. I don't want you. I found better. Leave me alone. Has anyone ever rejected you in a way that was hateful, hurtful and malicious?

See, there is a way that you can send people on their way without being nasty and wicked. (Genesis 21:8-21) YES!!! It might feel good to treat them like they did you....but you can't!!!!!

Remember, at your absolute best, you won't be good enough for the wrong person. At your absolute worst, you'll still be worth it to the right person. Fakes and frauds are unqualified.(Bishop Dale C. Bronner)

"For you formed my inward parts; you knitted me together in my mother's womb. I praise you, for I am fearfully and wonderfully made. Wonderful are your works; my soul knows it very well." (Psalm 139: 13-14)

APRIL 9

THE NEXT TIME YOU OPEN YOUR MOUTH

Life and death are in the power of the tongue. (18:21) Everything that you say has the power to bring forth or shut down. So, what are you saying?

I get it. It's easy to carelessly say things in casual conversation. But it doesn't matter. You're still speaking it into existence. For by your words you will be acquitted, and by your words you will be condemned. (Matthew 12:37)

It only takes ONE negative comment to KILL a dream. Remember that the next time you open your mouth! (Bishop Dale C. Bronner)

"Say to the righteous that it will go well with them, for they will eat

APRIL 10

YOU NEED TO STOP

You went to the altar and prayed but the next day you're back stressing, trying to work it out. But you turned it over to God. So, why do you keep having anxiety attacks and trying to fix it on your own? Now, that's not you, is it?

There comes a time that you must turn it over to the Lord and leave it there. (Psalm 55:22) If you keep taking it back you're telling God, you don't trust Him, and you don't have faith. (Proverbs 3:5)

Remember, if you try to change it, you will ruin it. Try to hold it, and you will lose it. (Lao Tzu)

"Those who trust in themselves are fools, but those who walk in wisdom are kept safe." (Proverbs 28:26)

_____

_____

_____

_____

_____

_____

_____

_____

_____

_____

APRIL 11

YOUR MIND IS YOUR OWN MIRROR

I'm just stupid. I'm too fat to do that. I don't have the looks for it. Surely that isn't you putting yourself down, is it?

You must know that life and death are in the power of the tongue. (Proverbs 18:21) So not only are you speaking what you are. But you're also giving it power.

Remember, your mind is your own mirror. You are what you think you are. Self-belief is one of the fundamentals of achieving success in life. (Dr Roopleen)

"Gentle words are a tree of life; a deceitful tongue crushes the spirit." (Proverbs 15:4)

_____
_____
_____
_____
_____
_____
_____
_____
_____
_____
_____
_____
_____
_____

APRIL 12

THE ENEMY HAS YOU RIGHT WHERE GOD WANTS YOU

John 10:10 tells us that the enemy comes only to steal, kill and destroy. And for many folks right now, they feel as if life is killing them because of what they're going through. But is it really?

You must learn to count it all joy when you're facing trials of various kinds. (James 1:2) YES! It might feel as if it's killing you. However, what the enemy means for evil, God is working for your good. (Genesis 50:20)

Remember, don't be disheartened by the forces of evil. Nothing can happen that God hasn't allowed. Even resistance is all part of grand orchestration. The devil always has you right where God wants you. (Steve Maraboli)

"I have told you all this so that you may have peace in me. Here on earth you will have many trials and sorrows. But take heart, because I have overcome the world."" (John 16:33)

APRIL 13

BIG TREES OUT OF SMALL SEEDS

Doubt is a feeling of uncertainty or lack of conviction. So, how many of you are feeling like that right now?

Fact is all you need is a mustard seed kind of faith and watch God work. (Luke 17:6) He needs to know that you have faith, trust and believe in Him and Him ONLY!!!

Remember, God calls big trees out of small seeds, so He prepares great monuments out of small minds. He will definitely call those wonderful things he put in you out of you. When He begins, do not resist. (Israelmore Ayivor)

""Because you have so little faith." He answered. "For truly I tell you, if you have faith the size of a mustard seed, you can say to this mountain, 'Move from here to there,' and it will move. Nothing will be impossible for you."" (Matthew 17:20)

APRIL 14

DILUTING YOUR TRUTH

I'm not good enough. I'm too fat. I don't think that I can do this. Is that you? Constantly putting yourself down and having self-doubt?

Truth is YOU ARE fearfully and wonderfully made. (Psalm 139:14) It's the enemy that's trying to creep in and attack your insecurities and make you think you are something that you're' not.

But thank God we know the devil is a lie!!! (John 8:44)

Remember, do not dilute the truth of your potential. We often convince ourselves that we cannot change, that we cannot overcome the circumstances of our lives. That is simply not true. You have been blessed with immeasurable power to make positive changes in your life. But you can't just wish it, you can't just hope it, you can't just want it... you have to LIVE it, BE it, DO it. (Steve Maraboli)

"For I can do everything through Christ, who gives me strength." (Philippians 4:13)

_____
_____
_____
_____
_____
_____
_____
_____
_____

APRIL 15

SOME BRIDGES NEED TO BE BURNED

Be careful don't burn your bridges. How many times have you heard that? The statement is true most of the time. However, there are some bridges that need to be burned.

Now am I telling you to act a fool when you leave a job, or a relationship ends suddenly? NO! Just as a dog returns to its vomit, so a fool repeats his foolishness. So, be wise!!! (Proverbs 26:11)

Remember, some bridges need to be burned because there are some places you should never return. (Bishop Dale C. Bronner)

""Do not call to mind the former things or ponder things of the past." (Isaiah 43:18)

APRIL 16

THE RIGHT TO REMAIN SILENT

Have you ever wanted to tell, pop and go off on someone that had so much to say about you? And what they were saying was lies that fueled the fire more.

I get it! You want to defend yourself. But you must learn to remain silent and let the Lord handle your foes. (Deuteronomy 3:22) What you can do is one thing ....and what God can do on your behalf, is another.

Remember, though silence is not necessarily an admission, it is not a denial, either. (Marcus Tullius Cicero)

""The LORD will fight for you while you keep silent."" (Exodus 14:14)

APRIL 17

HE CAN'T LIE

Do you know what it's like to be looked at in the face and be told a bold-faced lie? It hurts. No one wants to be lied too.

Paolo Coelho says, telling the truth and making someone cry is better than telling a lie and making someone smile. But do you know who won't lie to you? God! (1 Samuel 15:29)

YES! You're tired of trusting the wrong people and getting let down. But if you put you trust in God He won't fail you. (Titus 1:2)

Remember, God is not human, that he should lie. Nor does He change His mind. If He speaks it, He will act. If He promises, He will fulfill it. (Numbers 23:19)

"So, God has given both his promise and his oath. These two things are unchangeable because it is impossible for God to lie. Therefore, we who have fled to him for refuge can have great confidence as we hold to the hope that lies before us." (Hebrews 6:18)

APRIL 18

CHEERS TO MY PROBLEMS

Problems are a matter or situation regarded as unwelcome or harmful and needing to be dealt with and overcome. How many of you got problems right now? Well, cheers to them!

Because at the end of the day, problems are never going to go away. It doesn't matter if you have problems on your job, home or even in a relationship. But the good news is….all problems have an end date.

Remember, to every problem there is already a solution whether you know it or not. (Grenville Kleiser)

"I have said these things to you, that in me you may have peace. In the world you will have tribulation. But take heart; I have overcome the world."" (John 16:33)

APRIL 19

WITH EVERY GOOD DEED YOU ARE SOWING A SEED

Working in the Church. Giving Back. Volunteering. Is that you? If so, you are sowing seeds.

But don't be deceived: God isn't mocked, folks can also sow bad seeds too when they are wicked, mean, malicious and evil. So, don't let that be you. Because you will reap what you sow. (Galatians 6:7)

Remember, with every deed you are sowing a seed, though the harvest you may not see. (Ella Wheler Wilcox)

"The wicked earns deceptive wages, but one who sows righteousness gets a sure reward."   (Proverbs 11:18)

APRIL 20

WHO IS REALLY IN YOUR WAY?

What is that very special thing that you want to do? Now ask yourself, why aren't you doing it?

It's easy to make excuses and blame this person and money constraints. But sometimes the obstacles that we think are blocking us are really, US.

Remember, as long as a man stands in his own way, everything seems to be in his way. (Ralph Waldo Emerson)

"I thought about my ways and turned my steps back to your decrees." (Psalm 119:59)

APRIL 21

I GOT A BULLY

Most people think of mean and cruel kids in the school yard when they think of the word, bully. But a bully is a person who uses strength or power to harm or intimidate those who are weaker.

Truth is God's power is made perfect in weakness. (2 Corinthians 12:9) And the enemy can huff and puff all day long. But you have the Lord on your side. (Psalm 118:6)

Bottom line: God will not allow any person to keep you from your destiny. They may be bigger, stronger, or more powerful, but God knows how to shift things around and get you to where you're supposed to be. (Joel Osteen)

"But the LORD stands beside me like a great warrior. Before him my persecutors will stumble. They cannot defeat me. They will fail and be thoroughly humiliated. Their dishonor will never be forgotten." (Jeremiah 20:11)

APRIL 22

THIS IS LIKE A FAIRY TALE

A fairy tale ending would be great for a lot of stories in our lives. But the truth is our everyday life is often filled with the "other" kind of fairy tales – the ones that are so wild, they're hard to believe.

Life can get so crazy and out of control that even Lifetime Movie Network couldn't write that type of script. So, what do you do?

Well, you don't get weary in well doing and give up. (Galatians 6:9) Yes, it's hectic and crazy right now, but God is not leaving you in the forest alone. He is right there with you fighting on your behalf. (Exodus 14:14)

Remember, fairy tales are more than true: not because they tell us that dragons exist, but because they tell us that dragons can be beaten. (Neil Gaiman)

"Do not be afraid of them; the LORD your God himself will fight for you."" (Deuteronomy 3:22)

_____

_____

_____

_____

_____

_____

_____

_____

_____

APRIL 23

BE A KITE

Nasty, gusty, freezing winds. Just the thought of that type of blast coming your way can make you want to hibernate – just stay inside where it's always nice and warm.

But that is how folks react when opposition arises in their life. It feels like that wind has knocked the life right out of you. But has it really?

Truth is what you think is designed to come against you is really a set up to elevate you. (Genesis 50:20)

Rise above that opposition because God has given you the inner strength to soar like a kite.

Remember, kites rise highest against the wind - not with it. (Winston Churchill)

APRIL 25

THE THIEF OF TIME

I'll do it later, but not right now. Tomorrow, I'll make time to get to it. Is that your story?

See, what you're doing is called procrastination. You're just delaying and postponing the task at hand.

You keep telling yourself that you're going to get to it and do it. But for whatever reason, that day never comes.

Remember, never do tomorrow what you can do today. Procrastination is the thief of time. (Charles Dickens)

"The soul of the sluggard craves and gets nothing, while the soul of the diligent is richly supplied." (Proverbs 13:4)

APRIL 26

THE WOLF REALLY AIN'T THAT BIG

When you think of a wolf you think of a big bad animal with huge fangs that can come and attack you. But how many of you can relate to a "wolf" in your life currently?

Fact is it really doesn't matter where you're dealing with your "wolf" at. They can huff and puff all day long. But at the end of the day they still can't blow your house down.

Remember, this German proverb: fear makes the wolf bigger than he is.

"The LORD is on my side; I will not fear. What can man do to me?" (Psalm 118:6)

APRIL 27

DEUCES

In the urban dictionary the word deuces symbolize the "peace" sign when leaving an establishment. But how many of you want to give deuces to some folks in your life now?

There comes a point in your life that you have to say goodbye, arrivederci, sayonara and deuces. God is trying to bless you with new and better, but you're stuck on what was. (Isaiah 42:9) It's time to let it go!!!!

Remember, surrender to what is. Let go of what was. Have faith in what will be. (Sonia Ricotti)

""Remember not the former things, nor consider the things of old. Behold, I am doing a new thing; now it springs forth, do you not perceive it? I will make a way in the wilderness and rivers in the desert." (Isaiah 43:18-19)

APRIL 28

WHAT'S ON THE INSIDE?

Have you ever picked up a ripe banana and started to peel back the layers and it was rotten? Unfortunately, that's how folks can be.

You can see a beautiful woman or a handsome man on the outside. But once you get to know them you discover that beauty doesn't rest on the inside too.

Remember, people are often attracted to others by what they see on the outside; but people are often repulsed by what they discover on the inside! (Bishop Dale C. Bronner)

"For the Lord sees not as man sees: man looks on the outward appearance, but the Lord looks on the heart."" (1 Samuel 16:7)

APRIL 29

RUNNING OUT OF GAS

How does this look? Do you think I can do this? What about this look? Are you that person that is constantly looking for the approval and opinions from others?

The question that you must ask yourself is, why do you care? More importantly, do you like what you're trying to pitch?

If you fuel your journey on the opinion of others, you are going to run out of gas. (Steve Maraboli)

"It is dangerous to be concerned with what others think of you, but if you trust the LORD, you are safe." (Proverbs 29:25)

APRIL 30

A BLACKOUT

A blackout normally occurs when an electrical power supply has been out. However, there are folks now that feel as if they are living in the blackest and darkest times of their lives.

You might feel as if you're living in the dark and desperately wanting to see sunlight. But the Son is shining on you. (Numbers 6:25) Just walk by faith and not by sight, and you will see that your daylight is here!!! (2 Corinthians 5:7)

Remember, if patience is worth anything, it must endure to the end of time. And a living faith will last in the midst of the blackest storm. (Mahatma Gandhi)

"For God, who said, "Let light shine out of darkness," made his light shine in our hearts to give us the light of the knowledge of God's glory displayed in the face of Christ." (2 Corinthians 4:6)

_____
_____
_____
_____
_____
_____
_____
_____
_____
_____

MAY 1

OMG!!! WHAT AM I GOING TO DO?

Have you ever been in dire need of help? I mean you've tried everything that you can possibly think of. Yet still, you're stuck and in trouble?

That's going to happen when you try to fix things on your own. However, once you learn to turn all your worries, problems and troubles over to the Lord,(1 Peter 5:7) that anxiety and stress you have will cease and desist.

Remember, do not be anxious about anything, but in everything by prayer and supplication with thanksgiving let your requests be made known to God. And the peace of God, which surpasses all understanding, will guard your hearts and your minds in Christ Jesus. (Philippians 4:6-7)

So, stop stressing and give it over to the Lord!!!!

"Cast your burden on the Lord, and He will sustain you; He will never permit the righteous to be moved." (Psalm 55:22)

_____
_____
_____
_____
_____
_____
_____
_____

MAY 2

DO YOU REALLY THINK THAT'S A GOOD IDEA?

Folks make permanent decisions based on temporary feelings all the time. An argument and miscommunication can lead to a break up. A misunderstanding can leave a person walking out on their job. It's time to ask yourself, was that a good idea?

You can't react negatively every time something doesn't go your way. You must be still and watch the deliverance of the Lord on your behalf. (Exodus 14:13)

Remember, never cut a tree down in the wintertime. Never make a negative decision in the low time. Never make your most important decisions when you are in your worst moods. Wait. Be patient. The storm will pass. The spring will come. (Robert H. Schuller)

"Wise people think before they act;" (Proverbs 13:16)

MAY 3

SOME CHANGES LOOK NEGATIVE

Change can be hard to do and hard to take. However, everything isn't how it appears either. Salt can look like sugar and sugar can look like salt.

Fact is when changes come in your life you must embrace them. From the surface, things might appear negative and might not be what you want. But be still and wait patiently for The Lord. (Psalm37:7)

Remember, some changes look negative on the surface, but you will soon realize that space is being created in your life for something new to emerge. (Eckhart Tolle)

""But forget all that--it is nothing compared to what I am going to do. For I am about to do something new. See, I have already begun! Do you not see it? I will make a pathway through the wilderness. I will create rivers in the dry wasteland." (Isaiah 43:18-19)

_____
_____
_____
_____
_____
_____
_____
_____
_____
_____

MAY 4

STORMY WEATHER

Life can sometimes feel like a storm. Rough and raging winds throw you every which way. And powerful raindrops fall on you, cutting you like a knife. Sound familiar?

Well, keep this in mind. No matter how big or how wide a storm is, it must come to a stop at some point. Some storms you battle through may last just an hour, some for a day. And then, there will be those storms that linger for days on end. But rest assured, all of those storms, big and small, will come to an end.

Remember, if you want to see the sunshine, you have to weather the storm. (Frank Lane)

Your Storm is Ending!!!!!!!!!!!!

"Jesus responded, "Why are you afraid? You have so little faith!" Then he got up and rebuked the wind and waves, and suddenly there was a great calm." (Matthew 8:26)

MAY 5

DON'T BURN YOUR OPPORTUNITIES FOR A TEMPORARY COMFORT

You know he or she is taken. And you know you can't have sweets, but that sweet potato pie is calling your name. How many times have you been told to stop eating red meat? But that steak and gravy looks oh so yummy. Sound familiar?

We've all been there. Sometimes, we're there a lot. You know you have no business doing something. However, you do it anyway because it feels so good to do it. It's comfort! But is it worth the consequences?

Remember, it's a fool who will be stuck in a cold hole with a ladder and will cut the steps on the ladder to use for fire wood. He could have climbed the ladder to get out the hole, but he wanted that temporary comfort because he was cold.

Moral of the story: Don't Burn Your Opportunities for A Temporary Comfort.

"No temptation has overtaken you that is not common to man. God is faithful, and He will not let you be tempted beyond your ability, but with the temptation He will also provide the way of escape, that you may be able to endure it." (1 Corinthians 10:13)

_____
_____
_____
_____
_____

MAY 6

BAG LADY, BAG MAN

Baggage. And I'm not talking about the baggage that you have when you're about to travel. I'm talking about past experiences or long-held ideas regarded as burdens and impediments. How many of you have baggage that you need to unload?

There comes a time that you must stop walking around with all those bags dragging you down. Truth is they are causing damage and harm to your back. So, why are you carrying them?

Remember, future successes can be diminished by carrying baggage from the past. Let go of the excess baggage.   (Reed B. Markham)

"I cannot carry all these people by myself; the burden is too heavy for me." (Numbers 11:14)

MAY 7

WHY DO I HAVE TO GO THROUGH THIS?

Why am I going through this? Why God? Why? How many of you keep asking God that question right now?

It seems every which way you turn you're being attacked. But instead of asking God, why? Start thanking Him and praising for the storm and affliction you're going through. (James 1:2)

See you're a bank. And you have so much treasure and gold in you that the enemy wants it. (Deuteronomy 7:6) And you know the enemy comes to steal, kill and destroy. (John 10:10) But you have a "guard" all around you that has a hedge of protection covering you. (Job 1:10) So, the enemy can come. But he can't take what's in you. (Psalm 91:7)

Remember, character cannot be developed in ease and quiet. Only through experience of trial and suffering can the soul be strengthened, ambition inspired, and success achieved. (Helen Keller)

"We are pressed on every side by troubles, but we are not crushed. We are perplexed, but not driven to despair. We are hunted down, but never abandoned by God. We get knocked down, but we are not destroyed." (2 Corinthians 4:8-9)

_____
_____
_____
_____
_____
_____
_____

MAY 8

IT DOESN'T MAKE IT RIGHT

Well, they're doing it. So, I'll do it too. He did this to me, so I'm going to do this to him. Tit for tat. Now, that's not you, is it?

Yes, what they did is dead wrong. But trying to do unto others what they did to you doesn't make it right. (Leviticus 19:18) You must learn to let the Lord fight for you and be still. (Exodus 14:14)

That's easier said than done, but have faith. Do not be afraid; do not be discouraged. Go out to face them tomorrow, and the Lord will be with you. (2 Chronicles 20:17)

Remember, what is right is not always popular, and what is popular is not always right, (Albert Einstein)

"Do not take revenge, my dear friends, but leave room for God's wrath, for it is written: "It is mine to avenge; I will repay," says the Lord." (Romans 12:19)

_____
_____
_____
_____
_____
_____
_____
_____
_____
_____

MAY 9

YOU CAN'T CROSS THE SEA BY STARING AT THE WATER

Wanting and doing are two different things. Are you going to sit around and keep telling folks about your dream, or are you going to get up and do something about it?

Today, it's time to stop talking about what you're going to do and actually do it! You have the vision. So, write the plan and run with it. (Habakkuk 2:2)

Remember, you can't cross the sea merely by standing and staring at the water. (Rabindranath Tagore)

"Lazy people want much but get little, but those who work hard will prosper." (Proverbs 13:4)

_____
_____
_____
_____
_____
_____
_____
_____
_____
_____
_____

MAY 10

THAT TONGUE OF YOURS IS THE ENEMY OF THE SOUL

Just because you think it doesn't mean it needs to be said. Often, are mouths write checks that we just can't cash.

Today, you have to stop standing with your foot in your mouth. Everything foolish doesn't need a response.

Remember, listen! Clam up your mouth and be silent like an oyster shell, for that tongue of yours is the enemy of the soul, my friend. When the lips are silent, the heart has a hundred tongues. (Rumi)

"Those who control their tongue will have a long life; opening your mouth can ruin everything." (Proverbs 13:3)

MAY 11

A DIFFICULT EXAM

When you think of the word "exam", you probably think about a formal test of a person's knowledge in a particular subject or skill. But have you ever thought about how life is like a test?

Every day, you will be faced with challenges on every side. But just because things are getting hard and you don't understand it doesn't mean you throw your pencil down and stop. (Proverbs 3:5-6)

Just pick yourself back up. And hold on tight to God's unchanging hand, and press toward the mark. (Isaiah 41:13) (Philippians 3:14)

Remember, life is the most difficult exam. Many people fail because they try to copy others, not realizing that everyone has a different question to answer.

"We are hunted down, but never abandoned by God. We get knocked down, but we are not destroyed." (2 Corinthians 4:9)

_____
_____
_____
_____
_____
_____
_____
_____
_____
_____

MAY 12

WHY ARE YOU ALWAYS PICKING ON ME?

Picking. Kicking. Throwing. Do you know someone like that? It seems that no matter how you try to avoid them, they always find a way to throw rocks and hide their hands.

Fact is God says touch not my anointed ones, do my prophets no harm. (Psalm 105:15) See, don't cry, stress and get all worked up on a fool. And YES, they are fools because a fool is a person who acts unwisely. And the way of a fool is right in his own eyes. (Proverbs 12:15) Unfortunately, they see nothing wrong with their actions...YET!

You just keep on living, and don't you dare give up. And stop trying to get payback and do tit for tat too. (Galatians 6:9) Truth is the Lord saw and sees all. (Hebrews 4:13) It is Him who will avenge the wrongs that have been done to you. (Romans 12:19) All you must do is sit back and watch the deliverance of the Lord on your behalf. (Exodus 14:13)

Remember, every rock, stick and stone thrown at you? God saw it and is handling it for YOU!!!!

"'Vengeance is Mine, and retribution. In due time their foot will slip; For the day of their calamity is near, And the impending things are hastening upon them.'" (Deuteronomy 32:35)

_____
_____
_____
_____
_____
_____

MAY 13

IT HAD TO TAKE ALL THAT

The Pain. Hurt. Fear. Heartbreak. It was a lot to endure. Some days it felt as if you would never make it through. However, weeping may endure for a night, but joy does come in the morning. (Psalm 30:5)

So, YES! You've endured affliction. But had you not gone through that you wouldn't be the strong warrior that you are today. They meant it for evil, but God meant it for your good. (Genesis 50:20)

Remember, sometimes it takes sadness to know happiness, noise to appreciate silence and absence to value presence. (Bishop Dale C. Bronner)

"Yet what we suffer now is nothing compared to the glory He will reveal to us later." (Romans 8:18)

_____
_____
_____
_____
_____
_____
_____
_____
_____
_____

MAY 14

WHAT I DID, WHAT I DIDN'T DO, & WHAT I SHOULD'VE DONE

Shoulda. Coulda. Woulda. That is the story of many folks' lives. You can beat yourself up all day long about what you wish you had done differently, but that's all in the past. You have to leave it there and move forward.

There comes a time in your life you must accept the fact that the past is over. Everything happened the way it was supposed to. You may not like the outcome. But it all happened for a reason. It's over!!!

Make this declaration today and move on: I Refuse to Allow What I Did, What I Didn't Do, Or What I Should've Done, to Affect What I'm About to Do!

"Brothers and sisters, I do not consider myself yet to have taken hold of it. But one thing I do: Forgetting what is behind and straining toward what is ahead," (Philippians 3:13)

MAY 15

BUT I GOTTA SAY IT

Have you ever wanted to tell off someone and just let them know how you feel? What about that job that you've worked hard on for years and you put in the dedication and one day they tell you they are laying you off? OUCH!

But cursing and telling them how you feel will do what? Sometimes you must know when to speak and when to keep quiet. Not everything or everybody needs a response.

Remember, knowledge is knowing what to say. Wisdom is knowing when to say it. (Unknown)

"He who guards his mouth and his tongue, Guards his soul from troubles." (Proverbs 21:23)

MAY 16

YOU HAVE NOTHING TO BE ASHAMED ABOUT

Ashamed. Guilty. Embarrassed. Afraid of what others think. Is that your story?

Today is the day that you pick your head back UP!!!!!!!! Stop being ashamed about how someone sees you and be proud about who you are!!!!! You are not your past and you are not what others say you are. But you are a child of the most high. (Psalm 82:6) Walk like you know who you are!!!!!

Remember, never bend your head. Always hold it high. Look the world straight in the eye. (Helen Keller)

"Yet if anyone suffers as a Christian, let him not be ashamed, but let him glorify God in that name." (1 Peter 4:16)

_____
_____
_____
_____
_____
_____
_____
_____
_____
_____
_____

MAY 17

BURIED ALIVE

I feel like I am being buried alive. That is a phrase that is often used when life throws overwhelming blows back to back. When you think of not breathing it frightens people. Thoughts of being enclosed in a narrow space with one's breathing air diminishing, helpless, and unable to escape. How many wishes they can escape life's trouble right now?

Fact is weeping may endure for a night, but joy comes in the morning. (Psalm 30:5) Is this hard? YES!! The hurt, pain and the difficulty that you're going through right now is hard. However, God has you wrapped up in His arms. (1 Corinthians 16:23)

Remember, sometimes when you're in a dark place you think you've been buried, but actually you've been planted. (Christine Caine)

"They will be like a tree planted by the water that sends out its roots by the stream. It does not fear when heat comes; its leaves are always green. It has no worries in a year of drought and never fails to bear fruit."" (Jeremiah 17:8)

_____

_____

_____

_____

_____

_____

_____

_____

MAY 18

LET EM' KEEP TOUCHING THE STOVE

This isn't good for you. You need to leave. It's not healthy for you. It's time for you to go. Have you found yourself saying the same thing over and over to someone before?

See, Albert Einstein calls that insanity. Doing the same thing over and over again, but expecting different results.

Truth is you can't make others do anything. YES! It's hurtful and painful to see someone you love in pain. But sometimes you have to keep letting them touch the stove until they get tired of getting burned.

Remember, it is difficult to free fools from the chains they revere. (Voltaire)

"Like a dog that returns to his vomit is a fool who repeats his folly." (Proverbs 26:11)

MAY 19

OUT OF MY CONTROL

There are a lot of ways that people take control and use it to be in control. But what happens when you can't control the situation or diagnosis because it's out of your hand?

Truth is God knew you before you were born, and He knows how the story is going to end. (Jeremiah 1:5) And while you're running all over trying to handle everything stressing yourself out. God is already working it out.

Remember, our anxiety does not come from thinking about the future, but from wanting to control it. (Khalil Gibran)

"Do not be anxious about anything, but in everything by prayer and supplication with thanksgiving let your requests be made known to God." (Philippians 4:6)

MAY 20

AN EXTRAORDINARY MOVE OF GOD

What do you do when the prayers that you've been praying and asking God for are finally answered? Are you going to forget your obedience or are you going to continue to stand in faith and trust God to move in your life?

Just because you see a shift and things are looking up doesn't mean that you should stop praying, being obedient and trusting God. Don't think of God like a genie in a bottle. Trust Him all the time and He will do exceedingly above all things that you can even ask or think. (Psalm 37:5) (Ephesians 3:20)

Remember, an extraordinary move of God simply begins with an ordinary act of obedience! (Bishop Dale C. Bronner)

"If you are willing and obedient, you shall eat the good of the land;" (Isaiah 1:19)

_____
_____
_____
_____
_____
_____
_____
_____
_____
_____

MAY 21

PREPARE A VICTORY SPEECH

What you say has power. (Proverbs 18:21) So, if you think you will lose you're speaking defeat into existence. But think of the power you have if you keep telling yourself YOU WIN.

Today, it's time to make your dream a reality. Speak everything you want to come to pass as if it was happening NOW!!!!

Remember, never expect to lose. Even when you're the underdog, still prepare a victory speech.

(H. Jackson Brown, Jr.)

"Tell the righteous that it shall be well with them, for they shall eat the fruit of their deeds." (Isaiah 3:10)

MAY 22

THE BLUEPRINT

I want to stay. I need to go. Oh, I just don't know. Sound familiar?

It's frustrating not knowing what your next move is going to be. But keep this in mind: "Trust in the Lord with all your heart and lean not on your own understanding. In all your ways, submit to Him, and He will make your paths straight." (Proverbs 3:5-6)

Remember, hope is the blueprint. Faith is the building material. The enemy is after your hope, not just your faith. (Bishop Dale C. Bronner)

So, stay strong and believe!

"Through him, we have also obtained access by faith into this grace in which we stand, and we rejoice in hope of the glory of God." (Romans 5:2)

MAY 23

YOU'RE STILL VALUABLE

They left you. They said they didn't want you. They said that they were going to get better. Now, you're sad and depressed. NO! Now you say, Goodbye!!

Never let what others say or do to you devalue your worth or diminish it. Fact is God will never leave or forsake you. (Deuteronomy 31:6) And at the end of the day, He is all you need. (Philippians 4:19)

Remember, your value doesn't decrease based on someone's inability to see your worth. (Ted Rubin)

"For you are a people holy to the LORD your God. The LORD your God has chosen you out of all the peoples on the face of the earth to be his people, his treasured possession." (Deuteronomy 7:6)

MAY 24

DON'T LET YOUR GIFT TAKE YOU WHERE YOUR CHARACTER WON'T KEEP YOU

Beautiful. Talented. Gifted. But has the nastiest attitude that you've ever seen. Better yet gets a new boo so now they don't come to church on Sundays. And let's not forget the person that gets a new ride and has to go to the car wash and spend money on rims and trinkets to floss in that they used to pay tithes with. Do you know someone like that? But that's not YOU right???

Fact is God giveth and taketh away too. (Job 1:21) No one should get too cocky or arrogant to think that God won't knock them down and remind them of their humbling beginnings. (Isaiah 13:11)

Remember, don't let your gift take you where your character won't keep you. (Kimberly Higgins Simmons)

"Pride comes before destruction, and an arrogant spirit before a fall." (Proverbs 16:18)

MAY 25

YOU'RE TOO FAMILIAR WITH THE WORD IMPOSSIBLE

OMG I don't think I can do this. I am in over my head. Why did I get started with this? Oh Lord what have I got myself into? Now surely that isn't you, is it?

Impossible means not able to occur, exist, or be done. And that is exactly what the enemy wants you to think. But thank God, we know the devil is a lie!!!!

Fact is you can do ALL things in Christ who gives you strength. (Philippians 4:13) Therefore, nothing is impossible with God. (Matthew 19:26)

Remember, one of the main weakness from which we suffer is too much familiarity with the word "impossible" (Napoleon Hill)

""Is anything too difficult for the LORD?" (Genesis 18:14)

"For nothing will be impossible with God."" (Luke 1:37)

MAY 26

I THINK I CAN, I THINK I CAN

Everyone knows the story of "The Little Engine That Could". However, there is a part of all of us in that story.

YES! Life has been challenging and it would have been easier to just throw in the towel. But sometimes you have to be like that little engine in the book and keep telling yourself "I think I can. I think I can."

And just know that God is always there helping you along the way. (Deuteronomy 31:6)

So YES, you can!!!!

Remember, sometimes you don't know what you can do until you have to do it. (Bishop Dale C. Bronner)

"I can do all things through Christ who gives me strength." (Philippians 4:13)

MAY 27

HE ORDERS YOUR STOPS TOO

Often, we can get so mad and frustrated when we don't get what we planned, prayed and hoped for. And then have the nerve to get an attitude thinking that God isn't listening or has forgotten about us.

Well, just like God will order your steps, He will also STOP your steps too. (Psalm 119:133) You can't be so quick to get bent all out of shape because it's not going the way YOU want. Fact is it's going how God has planned. (Jeremiah 29:11) YOU just can't see it yet.

Remember, you can make your plans, but the Lord will order your steps. (Proverbs 16:9)

"LORD, I know that people's lives are not their own; it is not for them to direct their steps." (Jeremiah 10:23)

MAY 28

CURRENT CONDITIONS

Stormy. Breezy. Icy. That can describe the weather conditions for many folks' lives right now. No matter which way they turn, they're facing the brunt of the storm.

They're in the midst of a "rainy season", but that "season" won't last forever.

Remember, your current condition is not your concrete conclusion. (Bishop Dale C. Bronner)

Have faith in Him and realize there is no reason to fear such storms.

"When Jesus woke up, he rebuked the wind and said to the waves, "Silence! Be still!" Suddenly the wind stopped, and there was a great calm." (Mark 4:39)

MAY 29

I WISH I WOULD HAVE

Regret, feeling sad, or disappointed over something that has happened or been done, especially a loss or missed opportunity. How many of you have regrets in your lives?

Truth is tomorrow is not promised. (James 4:14) So, it's time to let go of the hate, grudge and animosity that you have with someone.

Remember, dead people receive more flowers than the living ones because regret is stronger than gratitude. (Anne Frank)

"For godly grief produces a repentance that leads to salvation without regret, whereas worldly grief produces death." (2 Corinthians 7:10)

_____

_____

_____

_____

_____

_____

_____

_____

_____

_____

_____

_____

MAY 30

ALL NIGHT LONG

Have you ever been up all night worried about a person or situation that has you bound and caught up? No matter what you do you just can't get a good night's rest?

See, it's time to turn all of it over to the Lord. (1 Peter 5:7) Truth be told you're worried about the wrong thing. And the enemy ain't up worried about you not getting no sleep. So, why are you up anyways?

Remember, it is the trouble that never comes that causes the loss of sleep. (Chas. Austin Bates)

You have nothing to be worried about!!!! God has YOU!!!!!!!!!

"Do not be anxious about anything, but in everything by prayer and supplication with thanksgiving let your requests be made known to God. And the peace of God, which surpasses all understanding, will guard your hearts and your minds in Christ Jesus." (Philippians 4:6-7)

MAY 31

IT WASN'T MEANT FOR YOU

Crying. Banging on the door. Still trying to plead your case. Yet still, the door won't open. Sound familiar?

There are some doors that you need to leave shut. So, that means stop tapping, knocking and kicking on it. God closed it for a reason. And no matter how you try to break in. It's still going to remain closed, because the door isn't meant for you.

Remember, realize that if a door closed, it's because what was behind it wasn't meant for you. (Mandy Hale)

"He knows us far better than we know ourselves. That's why we can be so sure that every detail in our lives of love for God is worked into something good. God knew what he was doing from the very beginning. He decided from the outset to shape the lives of those who love him along the same lines as the life of his Son." (Romans 8:27-29)

STOP Questioning Him!!!!

JUNE 1

THE HELL OF UNHAPPINESS

Sad. Depressed. Stressed. Battle Weary. That's a lot for one person to carry. So why are you carrying it?

Truth is God says, "come to me, all you who are weary and burdened, and I will give you rest." (Matthew 11:28) So, the unwanted stress, worry and heartache that you're experiencing is uncalled for. You're trying to handle something that God wants you to hand over to Him.

Remember, God loves us too much to leave us in the hell of unhappiness that comes from trying to do His job. Into the slavish misery of our ladder-defined lives, God condescends. (Tullian Tchividjian)

"Cast your cares on the LORD and He will sustain you; He will never let the righteous be shaken." (Psalm 55:22)

_____
_____
_____
_____
_____
_____
_____
_____
_____
_____

JUNE 2

A PURPOSE BEFORE THEY HAD AN OPINION

The definition of an opinion is a view or judgment formed about something, but not necessarily based on fact or knowledge. And just because someone has an opinion doesn't stop YOU and your dream from pushing forward.

So, never let other people and their opinions stop you from reaching your destination. You must believe that the Lord will fulfill His purpose for your life. (Psalm 138:8)

Remember, you had a purpose before anyone had an opinion.

"For am I now seeking the approval of man, or of God? Or am I trying to please man? If I were still trying to please man, I would not be a servant of Christ." (Galatians 1:10)

JUNE 3

I'M NOT GOING TO JAIL

When you've been hurt and done wrong it can be devastating and hurt to the core. Especially when it comes from someone you love and didn't see coming.

So, does that mean you should lose your freedom and act a fool? NO!!! It's times in adversity and trials that you can't lose your cool. No matter what the enemy does to you always keep in mind who you are and whose you are. (Psalm 127:3-5)

Remember, the next time you think of showing out on someone ask yourself, "is it worth the jail time?"

"Do not take revenge, my dear friends, but leave room for God's wrath, for it is written: "It is mine to avenge; I will repay," says the Lord." (Romans 12:19)

JUNE 4

EVERYBODY'S AFRAID OF SOMETHING

God doesn't give you a spirit of fear. (2 Timothy 1:7) But you're scared that your secret will be revealed. You're scared of what will happen next and of the unknown. But I repeat: God doesn't give you a spirit of fear but of power, love and a sound mind. (2 Timothy 1:7)

With that being said, YOU have nothing to be afraid of!!!!!! Fact is, God is fighting for you and you must be still and watch the deliverance of the Lord on your behalf. (Exodus 14:14)

So, forget what "they" say and what "they" do. YOU got the Lord on your side!!! (Psalm 118:6)

Remember, stop being afraid of what could go wrong, and start being excited of what could go right. (Tony Robbins)

"For I, the LORD your God, hold your right hand; it is I who say to you, "Fear not, I am the one who helps you."" (Isaiah 41:13)

JUNE 5

IT'S OKAY…HE HEARS YOU

You Pray. You cry. You stand. You fast. You even go to the altar. Yet it feels like nothing is taking place in your situation. So, YOU think. Sound familiar?

See, everything isn't as it appears. Sure, it might look as if God is silent right now. And you might think that the enemy is winning. But the last shall be first and the first shall be last. (Matthew 20:16)

Remember, God has heard every cry for help and saw every tear you shed. He has seen EVERYTHING and will justify the wrongs on your behalf. All you need to do is be still. He hears YOU!!!! (Hebrews 4:13) (Exodus 14:14) (Deuteronomy 3:22)

"The LORD looks on the righteous, and He listens to their cries." (Psalm 34:15)

JUNE 6

AIDING AND ABETTING

Yes, you can have this. Yes, you can go there. Yes, I'll give this to you. YES! YES! YES! Unfortunately, that's all some folks hear. But what happens when you tell them NO?

There comes a time that you must stop aiding and abetting because you don't want to hurt someone's feelings. Truth is a "NO" is better than a "YES" sometimes.

Remember, when you say "Yes" to others, make sure you are not saying "No" to yourself. (Paulo Coelho)

"For each will have to bear his own load." (Galatians 6:5)

JUNE 7

THIS ISN'T YOUR STOP

A watched phone never rings. How many of you have heard that saying before?

It's not so much about waiting for the phone to ring as much as it is about the patience in the wait. Truth is, every good gift comes from God. (James 1:7)

Just because you want it now doesn't mean that it's your time to get it.

Remember, if a train doesn't stop at your station, then it's not your train. (Marianne Williamson)

"Be patient, then, brothers and sisters, until the Lord's coming. See how the farmer waits for the land to yield its valuable crop, patiently waiting for the autumn and spring rains. You too, be patient and stand firm, because the Lord's coming is near." (James 5:7-8)

JUNE 8

STOP TALKING ABOUT HOW BAD YOU FEEL

Good morning, how are you? Well, I'm not feeling good. My arthritis is acting up. My knees are bad. I can't get rid of this bad cough. I have more bills than I do money. And I hate my job. Are you familiar with those type of conversations?

I get it. I have daily issues too that I could whine about. And folks could sit around all day and swap stories about how bad things are in their lives. But what good would that do?

YES! You have pain in your body. But instead of complaining about the pain, declare and decree that you are healed in Jesus' Name. Speak it as if it was. (Mark 11:22-24)

Remember, stop talking about how bad you feel and start talking about how healed you are. (Bishop Daniel J. Richardson)

"So shall my word be that goes out from my mouth; it shall not return to me empty, but it shall accomplish that which I purpose, and shall succeed in the thing for which I sent it." (Isaiah 55:11)

JUNE 9

YOU DON'T HAVE TO LIKE ME

For whatever reason some folks just don't like you. They don't like the fact that every time you fall, you get back up. They don't like the fact that you are really broke by your bank account status, but you don't look or live like it. For whatever reason they just don't like you. How many can relate?

Truth be told who cares if they do or don't like you? Because at the end of the day they can't stop God's favor over your life. (Proverbs 3:4)

Remember, some people don't like you just because your strength reminds them of their weakness. Don't let the hate slow you down." (Thema Davis)

"No, despite all these things, overwhelming victory is ours through Christ, who loved us." (Romans 8:37)

JUNE 10

STOP CHASING FOLKS THAT DON'T WANT YOU

Have you ever been in a relationship or connected to someone? And suddenly, he or she decides that's it, they're done. So, just like that, you're left with the what's and why's.

Well, what you must do is let them go. You don't chase and run after who left and walked away from you trying to ask questions.

Always remember, God never ties your destiny to who left you but who remains or is called to you. (Bishop Dale C. Bronner)

"They went out from us, but they did not really belong to us. For if they had belonged to us, they would have remained with us; but their going showed that none of them belonged to us." (1 John 2:19)

JUNE 11

A MATTER OF PERSONAL TASTE

Nothing is going right. You are about to leave the church. Job stressing you out. Got more bills than you do money. Folks keep telling you to smile, but a grin is about all you're going to do. Now does that sound like you?

Whether you want to or not you must rejoice and be happy, even when you don't feel like it. (Thessalonians 5:16) Actually, that's when you have to do it the most. See, the enemy comes to kill, steal and destroy. (John 10:10) And that even means your joy and peace. So, don't let him take your cheer too.

Remember, being happy is a matter of personal taste. (Pierre Teilhard de Chardin)

"Taste and see that the LORD is good. Oh, the joys of those who take refuge in Him!" (Psalm 34:8)

JUNE 12

BUT I WANNA SMACK EM

They did you so low down and dirty. But yet they go around smiling and giggling and it looks like they're untouchable. So, YOU Think. Sound familiar?

Touch not my anointed and do my prophets no harm. (Psalm 105:15) Fact is YOU are a child of The Most High. (John 1:12) They really don't know who they are messing with. And although you could set, pop and go off. It's not for you to do. The Lord will handle your foes. You need only to be still. (Exodus 14:14)

Remember, be nice to people on your way up because you'll meet them on your way down. (Wilson Mizner)

"May the LORD judge between you and me. And may the LORD avenge the wrongs you have done to me, but my hand will not touch you." (1 Samuel 24:12)

JUNE 13

PEPSI OR COKE

Mocking the man with the limp and ugly scars. Laughing at the girl that is eating alone in a restaurant. Now, surely that isn't you making fun and humiliating others, is it?

Would you have laughed if you knew that the man with the scar almost died saving children from a burning building? Truth be told, you never know what someone is going through or what the situation is.

A dark soda in a clear glass can sit on a counter. One might say it's a Coke; another, Pepsi. But it's not until you taste it that you discover what it really is.

So, stop letting filthiness, foolish talk and crude joking, which are out of place. But instead let there be thanksgiving lifted instead. (Ephesians 5:4)

You may find that, like the Coke or Pepsi, you'll enjoy the discovery you've made. (Jim Abath)

""The secret things belong to the LORD our God, but the things revealed belong to us and to our sons forever," (Deuteronomy 29:29)

JUNE 14

ARE YOU GONNA GET UGLY WITH YOURSELF?

Disrespectful. Rude. Ugly. Mean. That's how bad-mannered some folks can talk with one another. Now, imagine if it's YOU that talks bad about your own self.

Fact is, life and death is in the power of the tongue. (Proverbs 18:21) And you have the very thing in YOU to tear down or bring up! So, what do you choose to do?

Remember, be careful how you are talking to yourself because you are listening. (Lisa M. Hayes)

"The words you say will either acquit you or condemn you."" (Matthew 12:37)

JUNE 15

I WANT IT MY WAY

Patience is the capacity to accept or tolerate delay, trouble, or suffering without getting angry or upset. How many of you can work on patience?

I get it. I am one too that struggles with this. We live in a world where you can get a lot instantly.

So, when you've been praying, standing and fasting for God to answer your prayers and it's delayed. It's frustrating. But God works on His time not yours!

Remember, God answers prayers, but He doesn't always answer it your way. (Lou Holtz)

"But if we hope for what we do not see, we wait for it with patience." (Romans 8:25)

JUNE 16

THIS IS DROWNING ME

Drowning is to suffocate and die through submersion in and inhalation of water. Unfortunately, that's how a lot of folks feel when trials and storms come in waves and they feel overwhelmed.

However, just because you are thrown in the water doesn't mean that you have to drown. Fact is God is with you holding you up, making sure that you don't sink. He has YOU!!!! (Deuteronomy 31:6)

Remember, you drown not by falling into a river, but by staying submerged in it. (Paulo Coelho)

"He said: "In my distress I called to the LORD, and He answered me. From deep in the realm of the dead I called for help, and you listened to my cry. You hurled me into the depths, into the very heart of the seas, and the currents swirled about me; all your waves and breakers swept over me." (Jonah 2:2-3)

JUNE 17

A TEMPORARY CONDITION

You might be in a bad position right now because you've lost. You thought that you had it in the bag. But BOOM!!! You were hit with a NO and the disappointment. Sound familiar?

Fact is you have to lose in order to win sometimes. Because what they meant for evil, God means for your good. (Genesis 50:20) And every door that closes on you isn't a form of rejection. But a time to rejoice! (1 Peter 4:12-13)

Remember, being defeated is often a temporary condition. Giving up is what makes it permanent. *(Marilyn Vos Savant)*

"And let us not grow weary of doing good, for in due season we will reap, if we do not give up." (Galatians 6:9)

JUNE 18

THE GRUDGE

Do you know what it's like to have someone do you so low down and dirty that just the thought of them makes you regurgitate? But they stroll around like they've done nothing to you at all.

Yes, I get it. But you can't curse folks out and lay hands on them. You've got to learn to hold your peace. (Exodus 14:14) At the end of the day, God sees all and knows all. (Hebrews 4:13)

And you holding a grudge and acting a fool isn't going to make God fix it any faster. (Ephesians 4:31-32)

Remember, when you hold a grudge, you want someone else's sorrow to reflect your level of hurt, but the two rarely meet. (Steve Maraboli)

"Dear friends, never take revenge. Leave that to the righteous anger of God. For the Scriptures say, "I will take revenge; I will pay them back," says the LORD." (Romans 12:19)

JUNE 19

STOP BITING THE BAIT

Picking. Kicking. Pushing. Bullying. Have you fallen victim to the enemy's wrath lately?

I get it. It seems like there is no justice when the enemy keeps getting away with murder. However, looks can be deceiving too.

See, the enemy might be sitting, looking high and mighty now. But rest assured, God is keeping and blessing you. And He's also handling your enemies too. (Genesis 22:17)

Remember, never bite the bait of nasty people to stoop to their level. Don't let them change who you are! (Bishop Dale C. Bronner)

"May the LORD judge between you and me. And may the LORD avenge the wrongs you have done to me, but my hand will not touch you." (1 Samuel 24:12)

JUNE 20

SACRIFICING YOUR PEACE

She has a nasty disposition and attitude. She knows God doesn't like ugly. Did you see how he acted? He knows better. Sound familiar?

Are you that person that is quick to talk about someone that is in the wrong with you or others? Truth is you're not God!!! You can't put a person in heaven or hell. It's not for you to handle or judge them. (Matthew 7:1-5)

So, you getting all worked up because others are out of order is doing nothing but upsetting you and taking your peace away.

Remember, don't sacrifice your peace trying to point out someone's true colors. Lack of character always reveals itself in the end. (Mandy Hale)

"Do not fret because of evildoers," (Psalm 37:1)

JUNE 21

A WORST SITUATION

It's bad. Really bad and no matter what people keep telling you they still don't understand how awful the situation is. Can you relate?

YES! You've been dealt a bad hand. But just because the cards you have don't look good, doesn't mean you won't win the game. Fact is God says, YOU WIN. (1 Corinthians 15:57) So no matter how dim and bleak the situation appears, YOU are an overcomer!!! (1 John 5:4)

Remember, we cannot change the cards we are dealt, just how we play the hand. (Randy Pausch)

"A horse is prepared for the day of battle, but the victory is from the LORD." (Proverbs 21:31)

YOU don't have to fight. God is fighting for YOU!!!! (2 Chronicles 20:15)

_____
_____
_____
_____
_____
_____
_____
_____
_____
_____
_____
_____

JUNE 22

THIS IS BOTHERING ME

Sleepless nights. Pillow soaked full of tears. Panic attacks. Sound familiar?

It sounds like worry. And no matter how much you worry what good will it do? Yes! You are bothered by the events that have unfolded.

However, don't be anxious about anything. Instead, by prayer and supplication with thanksgiving, let your requests be known to God.

Remember, don't let things bother you that are designed to better you!   (Bishop Dale C. Bronner)

"But seek first the kingdom of God and his righteousness, and all these things will be added to you. "Therefore, do not be anxious about tomorrow, for tomorrow will be anxious for itself. Sufficient for the day is its own trouble." (Matthew 6:33-34)

_____
_____
_____
_____
_____
_____
_____
_____
_____
_____

JUNE 23

I'VE BEEN INJURED

Have you ever had a minor accident and got cut or hurt in the process? And now you see an ugly scar there that reminds you of the incident.

Truth is we all walk around with scars that have happened in our lives. The difference is some folks have visible scars and others have internal wounds.

However, the scars don't define you. They just show what you've been through.

Remember, scars are not injuries. But it is a scar that has healed. And after your injury, a scar is what makes you whole. (China Miéville)

"He heals the brokenhearted and binds up their wounds." (Psalm 147:3)

JUNE 24

A BROKEN WING

In life things are going to occur unexpectedly. Making you wonder: what's your next move?

Well, just because the unforeseen has taken place. Doesn't mean life shuts down for you.

Truth is, God saw the suddenly and already knows you will be fine. (Jeremiah 29:11) So, stop panicking and just trust Him!!! (Proverbs 3:5)

Remember, never let a broken wing stop you from planning your next flight! You will heal and fly again! (Bishop Dale C. Bronner)

"But those who trust in the LORD will find new strength. They will soar high on wings like eagles. They will run and not grow weary. They will walk and not faint." (Isaiah 40:31)

JUNE 25

THANK GOD IT DIDN'T WORK

Crying. Depressed. Practically losing your mind. All because it didn't work out. Can you relate?

It's time to praise and thank God, they left and let you go!!!!! Truth is they did you a favor.

See, you got caught up in the dilemma. Which is God's way of disguising His purpose!!!

Remember, what they mean for evil, God's is working out for your good!!!! (Genesis 50:20)

So, praise NOW and cry later!!!!!! (Philippians 4:4)

"The LORD is their strength, And He is a saving defense to His anointed." (Psalm 28:8)

JUNE 26

MY BACK IS BREAKING

Don't pick up that child, he's too heavy. Your backpack has too much in it. It's going to hurt your back. Sound familiar?

When you carry a lot of weight on you, it can cause harm and damage to your back. However, that's how folks operate daily.

They take on things that they should give over to the Lord. (1 Peter 5:7) You say you trust Him, right? So, trust Him enough to carry the weight for you. (Psalm 37:5)

Remember, it's not the load that breaks you. It's the way you carry it. (C.S. Lewis)

"Cast your burden on the LORD, and He will sustain you; He will never permit the righteous to be moved." (Psalm 55:22)

JUNE 27

I GOT WEEDS IN MY GARDEN

When you think of a garden, you think of beautiful plants and flowers that grow there. The last thing you think of in a garden are valueless, wild, troublesome plants that grow profusely and are unwanted. In other words, you don't expect weeds.

Unfortunately, a lot of folks have weeds in their lives. But just because you have wild, troublesome weeds in your garden doesn't mean that your plants and flowers stop blooming.

Remember, don't let the tall weeds cast a shadow on the beautiful flowers in your garden. (Steve Maraboli)

"They are like trees planted along the riverbank, bearing fruit each season. Their leaves never wither, and they prosper in all they do." (Psalm 1:3)

JUNE 28

THEY'RE NOT ALWAYS DRESSED THE WAY YOU THINK

There is a misconception that the enemy comes wearing a red cape and pointy ears or dressed in all black. Negative. However, what is true, the enemy does come to steal, kill and destroy. (John 10:10)

Facts is, there are enemies who come to you in sheep's clothing, but inwardly they are ferocious wolves. (Matthew 7:15) So you must be alert and aware always. Because the enemy prowls around like a roaring lion looking for someone to devour. (1 Peter 5:8)

Remember, the devil is not as black as he is painted. (Dante Alighieri)

"Put on the full armor of God, so that you can take your stand against the devil's schemes." (Ephesians 6:11)

JUNE 29

A BIRD DOESN'T COMPETE WITH A PLANE

The definition of envy is a feeling of discontent or resentful longing aroused by someone else's possessions, qualities, or luck. Now it's time to be honest, is that you?

Surely not. Truth is, you shouldn't be envious of one another. (Galatians 5:26) And you don't know what it took for a person to get to where they are. The oil and anointing cost. (Luke 12:48)

Fact is God has placed a special gift in all of us. (1 Peter 4:10) So, you don't have to be envious of your neighbor's gift.

Remember, no bird ever looked at a plane in envy. (Iain Thomas)

"A heart at peace gives life to the body, but envy rots the bones." (Proverbs 14:30)

JUNE 30

YOU TOO WILL GET OUT OF OZ

Genesis 50:20 tells us that what the enemy means for evil, God means for our good. So, that horrible thing that you went through or that you might be going through, will work out in the end.

See, when you're going through, it's hard to see the rainbow at the end of the storm. But just like the story of Dorothy in Oz, she does go back home to Auntie Em. And you too will make it through this!!!

Remember, if nothing else, one day you can look someone straight in the eyes and say, "But I lived through it and it made me who I am today". (Iain Thomas)

"That's why I take pleasure in my weaknesses, and in the insults, hardships, persecutions, and troubles that I suffer for Christ. For when I am weak, then I am strong." (2 Corinthians 12:10)

JULY 1

IT DOESN'T MATTER HOW YOU FEEL

Miserable. Depressed. Completely unhappy. That's a bad place in your life to be. BUT GOD!!!!

YES! Things seem bad right now. And every time you turn around it's something. However, every time you turn around, God is right there too. (Deuteronomy 4:31)

Remember, no matter how bad you're feeling. God is still working.

"Do not be afraid or discouraged, for the LORD will personally go ahead of you. He will be with you; he will neither fail you nor abandon you."" (Deuteronomy 31:8)

_____
_____
_____
_____
_____
_____
_____
_____
_____
_____
_____
_____
_____

JULY 2

BUT THEY WON'T FORGIVE YOU

You've said you're sorry. You've repeatedly apologized. And they still won't forgive you. Can you relate?

It's okay. You've owned up to your mistake and asked for forgiveness. Truth is you've done your part. It's not up to you if they decide to forgive or not forgive you.

Remember, as long as you sincerely want to please God in your heart. You must first be in alignment with Him, and He is not going to hold your past against you.

"If anyone will not welcome you or listen to your words, leave that home or town and shake the dust off your feet." (Matthew 10:14)

JULY 3

I CAN'T LIVE WITHOUT IT

Driving yourself crazy. Thinking about it nonstop. The back and forth. Can you relate?

Truth is you "think" you can't go on without someone or something. But God has giving you dominion, authority and power. YOU win! It doesn't matter what schemes and tricks the enemy brings. You will withstand. (Luke 10:19)

Remember, whatever you cannot live without controls and dictates your life! When you learn to do without things, then you master those things so that you can live peacefully with them. (Bishop Dale C. Bronner)

"For we do not wrestle against flesh and blood, but against the rulers, against the authorities, against the cosmic powers over this present darkness, against the spiritual forces of evil in the heavenly places. Therefore, take up the whole armor of God that you may be able to withstand in the evil day, and having done all, to stand firm." (Ephesians 6:12-13)

_____
_____
_____
_____
_____
_____
_____
_____

JULY 4

YOU FAILED TO HEAL FROM IT

Healed. To become healthy again. How many of you "think" you're healed but you're still walking around sick?

Truth is you can have full blown pneumonia and think you're fine. Why? Because you took "some" of your antibiotics. So, now you're going to get up and go in and out of the air without being healed. NEGATIVE!!!

Folks, that's what we do every day in life. We think that we are healed and then we find out that we haven't recovered from what made us sick in the first place.

Remember, whatever you fail to heal from becomes the very thing that you act out of! Forgive. Let it go. Be Healed, in Jesus' name! (Bishop Dale C. Bronner)

"He heals the brokenhearted and binds up their wounds." (Psalm 147:3)

JULY 5

THE CONSEQUENCES

I got bills to pay this week, so I'm going to pay my tithes out of my next check. It's not really cheating. It was a little white lie. Can you relate?

Here's the thing - God cannot be mocked. What you sow you shall reap. (Galatians 6:7) Sin is SIN!!! There is no thing as a little sin.

Remember, you may choose your sin, but you cannot choose the consequences. (Jenny Sanford)

"What will happen when he finds out what you are doing? Can you fool him as easily as you fool people?" (Job 13:9)

JULY 6

IT'S RUINING EVERYTHING

Have you ever felt like you've had a bad day that eventually turned into a bad week? And before you knew it you had a bad month. Sound familiar?

Truth is there are going to be good days and bad days. But just because you come across one stump in the road. Doesn't mean that the rest of the drive will be bumpy too.

Remember, confine your failure and use it to propel your destiny! Don't let one bad moment ruin your day. Don't let one bad day ruin your week. Don't let one bad person ruin your life. (Bishop Dale C. Bronner)

"Though they stumble, they will never fall, for the LORD holds them by the hand." (Psalm 37:24)

JULY 7

DON'T FORGET TO TAKE YOUR VITAMINS

Vitamins. Are organic compounds that are essential for normal growth and nutrition in small quantities in the diet for the body. So, do you take vitamins?

I'm sure many of you are immediately thinking that I am talking about the vitamins that go in your mouth and are like a pill or chewable form. But we still need vitamins that are going to enrich our lives as well.

Always remember to take your Vitamins: Take your Vitamin A for ACTION, Vitamin B for Belief, Vitamin C for Confidence, Vitamin D for Discipline, Vitamin E for Enthusiasm!! (Pablo)

"'People do not live by bread alone, but by every word that comes from the mouth of God.'" (Matthew 4:4)

JULY 8

COMFORT TO DISCOMFORT TO GREATER COMFORT

Hate it. Miserable. Ready to go. Sound familiar?

Lord knows I understand. But tell yourself: "It could be worse". You must know that God allows things and puts you somewhere because He is stretching you.

YES! It's uncomfortable and it doesn't feel good. But the discomfort you feel now has a purpose. (1 Peter 4:12-13)

Remember, you go from comfort to discomfort to greater comfort. Don't stop! (Bishop Dale C. Bronner)

"Who comforts us in all our affliction, so that we may be able to comfort those who are in any affliction, with the comfort with which we ourselves are comforted by God." (2 Corinthians 1:4)

_____
_____
_____
_____
_____
_____
_____
_____
_____
_____

JULY 9

DON'T BE A BIRD OF A FEATHER

"Birds of a feather flock together". We've all heard that phrase before. So, ask yourself: Who am I associated with?

Truth is your "associating" determines your destination. Bad company corrupts good character. (1 Corinthians 15:33)

Remember, birds of a feather not only flock together, but they also fly to the same destination. (Bishop Dale C. Bronner)

"You may learn his ways and find yourself caught in a trap." (Proverbs 22:25)

JULY 10
DON'T STOP PRAYING

Trials. Tribulations. Worry. Stress. How many can relate? Truth is life for you right now isn't a crystal stair. But that doesn't mean it's going to stay that way.

YES! The storm is raging, and you don't know what to do. But what you shouldn't do is be anxious and fret yourself to hysteria. Instead, go into prayer and let your requests be known to God. (Philippians 4:6)

Remember, prayer does not change God, but it changes him who prays. (Soren Kierkegard)

"But if we hope for what we do not yet have, we wait for it patiently. In the same way, the Spirit helps us in our weakness. We do not know what we ought to pray for, but the Spirit himself intercedes for us through wordless groans." (Romans 8:25-26)

JULY 11

THIS CAN'T BE FINAL

Final. Coming to an end. Is that how you feel right now?

YES! Life isn't what you expected. The ups and downs have you on a roller coaster ride that makes you feel as if you will never get off.

But God promises to give you a future, hope and an expected end. (Jeremiah 29:11)

So, if things for you are out of control...don't fret. It's not the end.

"Many, O LORD my God, are the wonders which You have done, And Your thoughts toward us; There is none to compare with You. If I would declare and speak of them, they would be too numerous to count." (Psalm 40:5)

_____
_____
_____
_____
_____
_____
_____
_____
_____
_____
_____
_____

JULY 12

THE PAST IS A PLACE OF LEARNING

It happened. It's gone. It is what it is. That's how folks describe the past.

Fact is there is no reason to keep hindering and driving yourself crazy about something that you cannot change. But what you can change is the lesson that you learned from the past.

Remember, the past is a place of learning, not a place of living. (Roy T. Bennett)

"Brothers and sisters, I do not consider myself yet to have taken hold of it. But one thing I do: Forgetting what is behind and straining toward what is ahead," (Philippians 3:13)

JULY 13

DON'T LET THE DEVIL STEAL YOUR SHOUT

Psalm 150:6 says, "Let everything that has breath praise the Lord!" So, how many of you are praising Him, no matter what the situation?

YES! The struggle is real. You have more bills than money. You're robbing Peter to pay Paul. But, at the end of the day, you have to know God is attracted to your praise, not your problems.

Remember, are the problems real? YES! But God is real also. (Romans 1:20) & (1 Corinthians 8:6)

"I will praise the Lord no matter what happens. I will constantly speak of his glories and grace. I will boast of all his kindness to me. Let all who are discouraged take heart. Let us praise the Lord together and exalt his name." (Psalm 34:1-3)

JULY 14

THIS IS HOW I SEE IT

Redeemed. Restored. Healed. Victorious. Now, ask yourself: "How do I see me?"

Truth is the Lord has already told you that you're the head and not the tail. (Deuteronomy 28:13) So, there is no reason to keep speaking and seeing yourself in a way that God said you weren't! (Proverbs 18:21)

Remember, we see things not as they are, we see them as WE are. (Morrie Camhi)

Now, see yourself a WINNER. (1 Corinthians 15:57)

YOU WIN!!!!!!

"We see things imperfectly, like puzzling reflections in a mirror, but then we will see everything with perfect clarity. All that I know now is partial and incomplete, but then I will know everything completely, just as God now knows me completely." (1 Corinthians 13:12)

_____
_____
_____
_____
_____
_____
_____
_____
_____

JULY 15

THEY THINK I'M CRAZY

She can't do that. Now who does he think he is? See, that's how folks talk about you when you dream big and act upon it.

Truth is when you want something, and it seems out of reach. You have to activate that crazy faith. And know that God is telling you to write the vision; make it plain that you will run when you read it. (Habakkuk 2:2)

So, move forward and run with your dream.

Remember, don't worry if people think you're crazy. You are crazy. You have that kind of intoxicating insanity that lets other people dream outside of the lines and become who they're destined to be. (Jennifer Elisabeth)

"For still the vision awaits its appointed time; it hastens to the end—it will not lie. If it seems slow, wait for it; it will surely come; it will not delay." (Habakkuk 2:3)

JULY 16

WHY ARE YOU CALLING ME LORD THEN?

I have to figure it out. I'm going to fix and take care of it. I'll handle it. Sound familiar?

Now, surely, you're not that person that is still trying to do EVERYTHING. But then going to God crying and whining saying, "I don't understand why this is happening". (Proverbs 3:5-6)

Fact is, you have to turn it over to the Lord and LEAVE IT!!!! You say you trust Him. So, why are you still trying to do it? (Psalm 55:22)

Remember, why are you going to keep calling and going to the Lord if you're going to do it anyways?

STOP IT!!!!!!

"Why do you call me 'Lord, Lord,' and not do what I tell you?" (Luke 6:46)

_____
_____
_____
_____
_____
_____
_____
_____
_____
_____

JULY 17

IF YOU CAN GET THROUGH THAT, YOU CAN GET THROUGH THIS

It's the worst time of your life. You don't know how you're going to get out of this. And you just don't know what to do. Sound familiar?

Well, don't you remember the last time you thought the same thing? And what happened? God stepped in and showed out like He's done time and time again.

Never forget that God has brought you through before and He will bring you through THIS TIME too. So, make the decision to choose faith over fear. (Deuteronomy 31:8)

"He has delivered us from such a deadly peril, and he will deliver us again. On Him we have set our hope that He will continue to deliver us," (2 Corinthians 1:10)

JULY 18

SMILE! EVEN ON THE WORST DAYS

Folks smile when they are happy. But how many can say even on the bad days they still walk around with a smile on their face?

YES! Weary. Sad. Horrible and even fretful days are going to come. But a joyful heart is good medicine. (Proverbs 17:22)

Remember, anyone can smile on their best day. I like to meet a man who can smile on his WORST. (Lauren Graham)

"A glad heart makes a cheerful face, but by sorrow of heart the spirit is crushed." (Proverbs 15:13)

JULY 19

I'M GOING TO AVOID IT

Have you ever found yourself trying to avoid something? I mean no matter how much you try to keep from doing or seeing someone they keep showing up.

Well, it's time to face your "Goliath" (1 Samuel 17) God doesn't give you a spirit of fear. So, why are you afraid? (2 Timothy 1:7)

Remember, a person often meets his destiny on the road he took to avoid it. (Jean de la Fontaine)

"Watch yourselves, so that you may not lose what we have worked for, but may win a full reward." (2 John 1:8)

JULY 20

YOU'RE RESPONSIBLE FOR YOUR FUTURE

I wish I would have done it differently. That's the story of many folk's lives. They sit, wish and think about how they could go back and re-do something.

Today, you must know that everything happened the way it was supposed to. It might have caught you by surprise, but it didn't catch God by one. (Jeremiah 1:5 & 29:11)

Remember, we are made wise, not by the recollection of our past, but by the responsibility for our future. (George Bernard Shaw)

"Brothers and sisters, I do not consider myself yet to have taken hold of it. But one thing I do: Forgetting what is behind and straining toward what is ahead," (Philippians 3:13)

_____

_____

_____

_____

_____

_____

_____

_____

_____

_____

JULY 21

A BOX FULL OF CHOCOLATES

Life is like a box of chocolates and you never know what you're going to get. (Forrest Gump)

Some of us might get dark, happy and ugly chocolates. Truth is we don't know what tomorrow may bring. But whatever it brings, God is in it with us through it all. (Isaiah 41:10)

Mary Oliver says "Someone I loved once gave me a box full of darkness. It took me years to understand that this too was a gift."

So, no matter what chocolate you're given, God will always use it for your good!!!!

"As for you, you meant evil against me, but God meant it for good," (Genesis 50:20)

JULY 22

GIVE THE GIFT OF ABSENCE

Give. Give. Give. You've given so much that now you've made it a habit to be depended upon. But when it's time for YOU. No one is there to be found. Sound familiar?

Today, it's time to show folks your absence instead of your presence. Does that mean you don't care? NO! But it does mean that it's time to put YOU first for a change.

Remember, give the gift of absence to people who don't appreciate your presence. (Pastor Jamal Bryant)

"To acquire wisdom is to love oneself; people who cherish understanding will prosper." (Proverbs 19:8)

_____

_____

_____

_____

_____

_____

_____

_____

_____

_____

_____

JULY 23

….AND YOU WILL NEVER HAVE

Hmmm, well look at that. I don't know how they did it. Now, surely that isn't you, is it?

Hating, envy and jealousy don't look good or pretty on you. Truth is you don't know what it took for "them" to get it or to be where they are. So, why are you mad?

Remember, you will never have….what you hate to see others with! (Pastor Jamal Bryant)

"For where jealousy and selfish ambition exist, there will be disorder and every vile practice." (James 3:16)

JULY 24

I CAN'T! I'M SCARED

Fearful and frightened. That's how folks get when they start to get scared.

But, God doesn't give us a spirit of fear. (2 timothy 1:7) So, why are you afraid?

You must know that if you are afraid, it's not of God. That's the enemy trying to play tricks on you to make you doubt what God has for you to do. (Ephesians 6:11)

Remember, when you're scared, you stay as you are! (Stephen Richards)

"The LORD is my light and my salvation; whom shall I fear? The LORD is the stronghold of my life; of whom shall I be afraid?" (Psalm 27:1)

JULY 25

SHIPS ARE SAFE IN THE HARBOR

Safe. Protected from or not exposed to danger or risk; not likely to be harmed or lost. How many of you want to be safe?

YES! Who doesn't want to be safe? However, life is about risks and taking chances. Just because you fell in love with the "wrong one". Doesn't mean that you will never love again. The "right one" is there.... but until you step out on faith and try. You'll never know.

Remember, a ship is safe in harbor, but that's not what ships are for. (William G.T. Shedd)

"Then I proclaimed a fast there, at the river Ahava, that we might humble ourselves before our God, to seek from him a safe journey for ourselves, our children, and all our goods." (Ezra 8:21)

JULY 26

ACT LIKE YOU ALREADY WON

Happy. Joyful. Shouting. Cheering. That's how folks act when they win. But how do you act if you lose?

Win or lose, you're still victorious. (1 Corinthians 15:57) So, go ahead and shout like you've already won.

Remember, regardless of how you feel inside, always try to look like a winner. Even if you're behind, a sustained look of control and confidence can give you a mental edge that results in victory. (Arthur Ashe)

"Because your love is better than life, my lips will glorify you. I will praise you as long as I live, and in your name, I will lift up my hands." (Psalm 63:3-4)

JULY 27

I DON'T FEEL ANYTHING

Heartache. Pain. Loss. So, when the messenger comes and brings more bad news. You just become mute to it. Sound familiar?

YES! Life has been hard. It hasn't been a crystal staircase for you. But every difficulty, whether big or small....will be something God will use to produce more strength, faith and perseverance in you, if you let Him!

Remember, all your pain has a purpose.

"And after you have suffered a little while, the God of all grace, who has called you to His eternal glory in Christ, will himself restore, confirm, strengthen, and establish you." (1 Peter 5:10)

JULY 28

MOVE YOUR FEET

God please help me. God direct me where I should go. But you don't do anything with what He has given you. Now, is that you?

See, you can't keep asking God for guidance, direction and wisdom. And then He gives it to you...you don't do anything with it.

Remember, do not ask God to guide your footsteps, if you're not willing to move your feet.

"Be doers of the word, and not hearers only. Otherwise, you are deceiving yourselves." (James 1:22)

JULY 29

WATCH ME

You can't do that. You will never make it. That's how folks talk when they don't want to see you live the dream that's inside of you. BUT GOD!!!!

See, let "them" say whatever. But at the end of the day they aren't the ones that created you or know how the story will end. (Isaiah 43:1)

Remember, there are so many people out there who will tell you that you can't. What you've got to do is turn around and say, "Watch me."

"For I can do everything through Christ, who gives me strength." (Philippians 4:13)

JULY 30

YOU CAN & YOU WILL

I think I can. I think I can. I think I can. Say it over and over and YOU WILL.

Nothing in life is easy. There will be bruises, hurts and pains. But sitting on the sideline is just that. You're sitting and watching. Now, it's time to get in the game and play.

Remember, they can because they think they can. (Virgil)

"For I can do everything through Christ, who gives me strength." (Philippians 4:13)

JULY 31

NOTHING JUST HAPPENS

Suddenly you divorced. Suddenly they left. Suddenly you were let go. Suddenly the accident happened. Now what?

Now you continue to press toward the mark. (Philippians 3:14) At the end of the day "life" happens. Just because it's a surprise to you, doesn't mean it's a surprise to God.

So, heads held high and wipe the tears from your face. Because if it happened, God will use it and it will be for your good. (Genesis 50:20)

Dear friends, don't be surprised at the fiery trials you are going through, as if something strange were happening to you. Instead, be very glad--for these trials make you partners with Christ in his suffering, so that you will have the wonderful joy of seeing his glory when it is revealed to all the world. (1 Peter 4:12-13)

AUGUST 1

STOP THINKING ABOUT IT

2 Timothy 1:7 tells us that God doesn't give us a spirit of fear. But somehow, we still are fearful of the medical report, the court date, the interview and the phone call. So why?

It's time to release your fear and worries over to the Lord for He cares for you. (1 Peter 5:7) You don't have to be sitting worried about a thing.

Remember, if you want to conquer fear, don't sit home and think about it. Go out and get busy. (Dale Carnegie)

"Cast your burden upon the LORD and He will sustain you; He will never allow the righteous to be shaken." (Psalm 55:22)

AUGUST 2

THE WORST TIME OF MY LIFE

This is the worst time of my life. How many of you know that feeling?

It doesn't matter if yours isn't the level of the next person, but it still hurts and devastates you just the same.

But at the end of the day, this too shall pass.

Remember, I am not what happened to me, I am what I choose to become. (Carl Gustav Jung)

And YOU are an overcomer!!!!

"Blessed is the one who perseveres under trial because, having stood the test, that person will receive the crown of life that the Lord has promised to those who love Him." (James 1:12)

_____

_____

_____

_____

_____

_____

_____

_____

_____

_____

AUGUST 3

THE CURVE BALL THROWN

Often when life throws you a curve ball you have to be able to deal and adjust to it. So, there will be a lot of ducking, swinging and hard hits that might come. But you stay in the game.

Fact is that's when you start to get your brave on. Be courageous, strong and not dismayed at the trials you're enduring. For the Lord your God is with you through it all. (Joshua 1:9)

Remember, the beginning is perhaps more difficult than anything else, but keep heart, it will turn out all right. (Vincent Van Gogh)

"And we know that God causes everything to work together for the good of those who love God and are called according to his purpose for them." (Romans 8:28)

AUGUST 4

TORTOISE & THE HARE

You have a dream. But you don't have everything you need yet to make the dream happen the way YOU want. Does that mean you stop? NO!

It's time to see yourself as "Tortoise and The Hare". We all know the story. In case you don't, Tortoise is a slow turtle that wasn't as fast as bragging Hare that knew he would win the race. In the end Tortoise wins.

Pinch yourself right now and say, ALL I DO IS WIN!!!!! (1 Corinthians 15:57)

So, just because you might be small now and not as big and as fast as everyone else. Doesn't mean that you won't win the race.

Remember, great things are done by a series of small things brought together. (Vincent Van Gogh)

""For the vision is yet for the appointed time; It hastens toward the goal and it will not fail. Though it tarries, wait for it; for it will certainly come, it will not delay." (Habakkuk 2:3)

AUGUST 5

BUT I FELL DOWN YESTERDAY

In life you will fall and get back up. And then someone will kick, knock, push and slam you back on the floor. So, are you going to stay there? NO!

No matter how many times you fall, lose or get rejected. Keep on going and never stop or quit. (Galatians 6:9) GET BACK UP!!!!

Remember, if you fell down yesterday, stand up today. (H. G. Wells)

"For the righteous falls seven times and rises again," (Proverbs 24:16)

AUGUST 6

IT'S NOT THREE STRIKES

The definition of failure is lack of success. Let's face it, nobody wants to fail but sometimes it happens. However, the defeat doesn't define you.

Every so often you have to lose to win. What you think is failure God is just waiting to see how you're going to react to it? So, are you going to lay in the floor and bed forever upset about the loss? Or are you going to get back up and start swinging the bat again? (2 Corinthians 12:9)

Remember, it's how you deal with failure that determines how you achieve success. (Charlotte Whitton)

"Though the fig tree does not bud and there are no grapes on the vines, though the olive crop fails, and the fields produce no food, though there are no sheep in the pen and no cattle in the stalls, yet I will rejoice in the LORD, I will be joyful in God my Savior." (Habakkuk 3:17-18)

AUGUST 7

WHO ARE YOU TO JUDGE

The definition of judging is to form an opinion or conclusion about something. Unfortunately, folks judge all the time. They judge the woman with 5 kids and assume that she has 5 different fathers and on assistance. They judge the man that has long hair and baggy clothes. They judge the girl that wears tight fitting clothes. They judge the boy that wears skinny jeans. But the question is....Who are you to judge?

Truth is everybody has a story. And you don't know what a person went through to get to where they are now. So, what gives you the right to judge them?

What if the stage was set and the spotlight was turned on YOU? And everything you've done was being talked about, judged and criticized???? So, STOP!!!

Remember, judge not, unless you judge yourself. Judge not, if you're not ready for judgment. (Bob Marley)

"Do not judge, or you too will be judged. For in the same way you judge others, you will be judged, and with the measure you use, it will be measured to you." (Matthew 7:1-2)

_____
_____
_____
_____
_____
_____

AUGUST 8

THE ATTACK IS PROOF

Every day it seems like it's something. Job woes. Church drama. Relationship issues. Truth is the attacks keep getting stronger. So, now what?

Now, you count it all joy at the various trials that you're enduring. Because you know that when your faith is tested, your endurance has a chance to grow. (James 1:2-3)

Remember, attack is the proof that your enemy anticipates your success. (Mike Murdock)

You're made for the struggle....YOU got this!!!!!

"These trials will show that your faith is genuine. It is being tested as fire tests and purifies gold--though your faith is far more precious than mere gold. So, when your faith remains strong through many trials, it will bring you much praise and glory and honor on the day when Jesus Christ is revealed to the whole world." (1 Peter 1:7)

AUGUST 9

WHATEVA

Often life goes so peachy for you that you strut yourself right on and have an attitude and say so easily, "Whateva!" But, when you look back at your life you should say, Thank You God!!! Even with all the challenges, affliction, rejection, suffering and hard times, He still kept YOU. And will continue to keep you! (Hebrews 13:5)

If you're reading this now that means that you're still alive, despite all the attacks that tried to take you out!!!! So, never forget how far He has brought YOU!!! Don't get too cocky, arrogant or stuck up that you can't remember your humbling beginnings.

Remember, the higher we are placed, the more humbly we should walk. (Marcus Tullius Cicero)

"He lifted me out of the pit of despair, out of the mud and the mire. He set my feet on solid ground and steadied me as I walked along. He has given me a new song to sing, a hymn of praise to our God. Many will see what he has done and be amazed. They will put their trust in the LORD." (Psalm 40:2-3)

AUGUST 10

YOU CAN'T BE BEAT

Often, when you're in the race, no matter what the "race" is, you're going to get tired. And the enemy will try to get at you and throw fiery darts, trying to force you to give up. (Ephesians 6:16)

But you can't. That's when you have to press toward the mark even harder because the attack is going to get stronger. (Philippians 3:14) Is it easier said than done? YES! But you must press and fight on!!!! (1 Timothy 6:12)

Remember, you just can't beat the person who never gives up. (Babe Ruth)

"No discipline is enjoyable while it is happening--it's painful! But afterward, there will be a peaceful harvest of right living for those who are trained in this way." (Hebrews 12:11)

AUGUST 11

POWERFUL PRAISE FROM A PERSON IN PAIN

Have you ever been at the point that you're just tired? You get up only to get knocked back down. You try to press forward but the pressure is just too much to bear. Sound familiar?

When you feel like that, know that's when the tide is about to shift!!!! It's right when you feel like giving up that the enemy turns up the attacks to make you stop. (Galatians 6:9) But you rejoice, pray and praise through it all. (1 Thessalonians 5:16-18) Because a person in pain will come forward with a powerful praise. So, Praise on!!!!! (Psalm 150:1-6)

Remember, victory is always possible for the person who refuses to stop fighting. (Napoleon Hill)

"That is why I can never stop praising you; I declare your glory all day long." (Psalm 71:8)

AUGUST 12

COOL MORE THAN COLD WATER

You're' beautiful. You're ugly. You're stupid and will never amount to anything. You're wonderful and will be a blessing to the world.

As you can see, words are powerful. They can lift you up or they can tear you down.

What you say can ultimately determine how a person feels and what they do?   So, what are you saying?

Remember, good words cool more than cold water. (John Ray)

"The tongue can bring death or life;" (Proverbs 18:21)

Watch what you say!!!

AUGUST 13

YOU'RE A GREAT PEACH

In life, you will have some folks that like you and others that don't. Does that mean that your show stops because one doesn't want to be in the crowd? NO! You continue to perform.

Truth is, Jesus was mocked, wasn't liked, ridiculed and crucified. But He still arose! (Matthew 10:34 & 20:19)

Fact is YOU are arising and making your mark. But unfortunately, it can come with a level that means everyone isn't going to celebrate with or for you. So, higher the level, bigger devils.

Remember, you can be the ripest, juiciest peach in the world, and there's still going to be somebody who hates peaches. (Dita Von Teese)

"If the world hates you, know that it has hated me before it hated you. (John 15:18)

AUGUST 14

WHO'S GOING TO STOP YOU?

You want the business. You want the career. You see the dream. So, what's stopping YOU?

Truth be told "they," no matter how you see them -haters, enemies and doubters - can't stop your show. Only YOU can. SO, what are you waiting for?

God doesn't give us a spirit of fear, but of power. (2 Timothy 1:7) And everything you need is in YOU to push forward and birth your dream out. (Philippians 3:14)

So, the question isn't who is going to let me it's who is going to stop me. (Ayn Rand)

"For I can do everything through Christ, who gives me strength." (Philippians 4:13)

AUGUST 15

SOLDIERS TRIUMPH IN WAR

Affliction. Hard knocks. Calamity. A Catastrophe. Disaster. Suffering. They all total up to adversity.

Fact is, you will be afflicted in every way. BUT, after you have suffered a little while, the God of all grace who has called you to His eternal glory in Christ, will Himself restore, confirm, strengthen, and establish YOU. (1 Peter 5:10)

Remember, brave men rejoice in adversity, just as brave soldiers triumph in war. (Lucius Annaeus Seneca)

So, be truly glad. There is wonderful joy ahead, even though you have to endure many trials for a little while. These trials will show that your faith is genuine. It is being tested as fire tests and purifies gold-- though your faith is far more precious than mere gold. So, when your faith remains strong through many trials, it will bring you much praise and glory and honor on the day when Jesus Christ is revealed to the whole world. (1 Peter 1:6-7)

AUGUST 16

MAYBE YOU'RE THE REASON

Often when things aren't going our way we are quick to say, "It's the enemy and the devil attacking." But have you ever thought about your own actions might be causing the attack in the first place?

Fact is, you reap what you sow, and life and death is in the power of the tongue. (Galatians 6:7) (Proverbs 18:21) You can't go around and be nasty and wicked and think you're going to prosper. And if you keep saying negative words from your mouth, negative is what will come forward.

So, don't YOU be your enemy and the very reason to getting your blessings blocked!!!!

Remember, every day people block their own blessings with the negativity that they do, and don't even know it!

"Therefore, shall they eat of the fruit of their own way, and be filled with their own devices." (Proverbs 1:31)

AUGUST 17

AN ENTRY SOMEWHERE ELSE

When doors close, it's frustrating, heartbreaking and can be devastating. But that doesn't mean that's the end of the show. Despite how it looks, it's really the beginning.

No matter what you think is a loss. Just know that if God took, closed and even slammed it, He has better in store!

Remember, every exit is an entry somewhere else. (Tom Stoppard)

"For I am about to do something new. See, I have already begun! Do you not see it? I will make a pathway through the wilderness. I will create rivers in the dry wasteland." (Isaiah 43:19)

AUGUST 18

I DON'T FEEL LIKE IT

I don't feel like praying for them. I don't feel like going to church. I don't feel like being nice. Sound familiar?

Often, you have to do things that you don't want to do and that doesn't feel good. But that doesn't mean that you don't do it. Fact is that's when you must do it the most.

YES! Doing the wrong thing will make you feel good. But what will be the ultimate result and consequence? (Hebrews 4:13)

Remember, stress comes from knowing what is right. But doing what is WRONG!!!!!! (Larry Winget)

It's time to get it together!!!!!

"Yes, each of us will give a personal account to God." (Romans 14:12)

AUGUST 19

LEAN NOT TO THY OWN UNDERSTANDING

Why Lord, why? Have you ever had to say that because you just don't understand why "this" is happening?

Fact is don't be surprised at the fiery trials you're going through, as if something strange were happening to you.(1 Peter 4:12) Does it make sense or is it right? NO! BUT GOD!!!! (Ephesians 2:4)

Remember, time heals what reason cannot. (Lucius Annaeus Seneca)

"For still the vision awaits its appointed time; it hastens to the end—it will not lie. If it seems slow, wait for it; it will surely come; it will not delay." (Habakkuk 2:3)

"But trust in the LORD with all your heart, and do not lean on your own understanding." (Proverbs 3:5)

AUGUST 20

IMAGINATION VS. REALITY

Looking at the situation with your natural eyes, it looks bad. Folks are trying to tell you it's okay and it's not that bad. But you know they're not in your shoes and you know how awful the situation is. Sound familiar?

Fact is we walk by faith, not by sight. (2 Corinthians 5:7) Instead, of tripping and worrying about how dire it is, turn your anxiety and worry over to The Lord. For God is not going to let you sink and die in it. But He will take a hold of your right hand and say to you, "Do not fear; I will help you." (Isaiah 41:13)

Remember, we are more often frightened than hurt; and we suffer more from imagination than from reality. (Lucius Annaeus Seneca)

"I pray that the eyes of your heart may be enlightened in order that you may know the hope to which he has called you, the riches of his glorious inheritance in his holy people," (Ephesians 1:18)

AUGUST 21

AN IDIOT WILL PERSIST

An idiot is known as a stupid person. But a stupid person is someone that shows great lack of intelligence or common sense. Now is that you? Surely not!!!

Truth is, we all make mistakes. Some were harder lessons than others, but they are all lessons learned. However, it's up to YOU to decide if you will grow and go on from them or continue to repeat them.

Remember, any man can make mistakes, but only an idiot persists in his error. (Marcus Tullius Cicero)

"Like a dog that returns to his vomit is a fool who repeats his folly." (Proverbs 26:11)

AUGUST 22

THE GREATEST DISAPPOINTMENT

Being disappointed is when the feeling of sadness or displeasure caused by the nonfulfillment of one's hopes or expectations occur. No one wants to be disappointed. Unfortunately, no one can avoid it either.

However, what you think is a disappointment is a blessing in disguise. For nothing in this world is by chance. God knew you before you were even born and how your story will end. (Jeremiah 1:5) (2 Timothy 2:19) So, rest assure He has YOU!!!! (Psalm 121:7)

Remember, one's best success comes after their greatest disappointments. (Henry Ward Beecher)

"All discipline for the moment seems not to be joyful, but sorrowful; yet to those who have been trained by it, afterwards it yields the peaceful fruit of righteousness." (Hebrews 12:11)

_____
_____
_____
_____
_____
_____
_____
_____
_____
_____

AUGUST 23

YOUR RIDE OR DIE

The term, "Ride or Die" is a meaning that stems from the hip hop culture. It's a woman or man that is willing to support their partner and lifestyle, despite how this might endanger or harm them. But how many of you have so-called ride or die friends? And when it gets hot will they split??

Fact is the real Ride or Die is The Lord. For He says that He will never leave nor forsake you. (Deuteronomy 31:6) And He is not like man that He shall lie. If He said it, He will surely do it! (Numbers 23:19)

Remember, NEVER will He leave, and NEVER will He forsake YOU!!!!!! (Hebrews 13:5)

"A man of too many friends comes to ruin. But there is a friend who sticks closer than a brother." (Proverbs 18:24)

AUGUST 24

YOU'RE BEING POLISHED

Problems on the job, at home, in your relationship and battle weary at church. That's a bad combination when all of them are happening at once. So, what do you do?

Well, you don't get weary in well-doing. (Galatians 6:9) But you do continue to press on toward the mark. (Philippians 3:14) If you faint in the day of adversity, your strength is small. (Proverbs 24:10) And God says, you are more than a conqueror. (Romans 8:37) Truth be told, YOU'RE made for this!!!!

Remember, a gem cannot be polished without friction. Nor a man polished without trials. (Lucius Annaeus Seneca)

"We are afflicted in every way, but not crushed; perplexed, but not driven to despair; persecuted, but not forsaken; struck down, but not destroyed." (2 Corinthians 4:8-9)

AUGUST 25

HOW ARE YOU? I'M FINE!

How many times a day does someone ask how you're doing? And when they do, you shoot off with the standard robot reply, "I'm Fine". But you're not. You're actually dying inside. Is that you?

In times of adversity and affliction don't hide how you feel. Fact is that's when you need to call on The Lord. (Psalm 145:18) Even if all you can say is, God HELP ME!!!

Remember, stop hiding all your tears and scars behind, I'm Fine. Chances are, you're lying anyways.

"God is our refuge and strength, a very present help in trouble." (Psalm 46:1)

"Ask, and it will be given to you; seek, and you will find; knock, and it will be opened to you." (Matthew 7:7)

AUGUST 26

ARE YOU WEARING YOUR HEARTACHE LIKE THORNS?

Are you broken-hearted? And I'm talking about the kind of heartbreak that you just don't know how you will ever recover from.

Well, heartache is painful. And if we aren't careful we can't inflict the pain we feel unto others.

Remember, all too often we wear our heartache like thorns and the people that love us bleed out just trying to wrap their arms around us. It's just not right when we make others bleed for our own pain. (Dave Wise)

This too shall pass. So, don't hurt others because you're hurting!

"The Lord is near to the brokenhearted and saves the crushed in spirit." (Psalm 34:18)

AUGUST 27

I'M TIRED OF DOING THE RIGHT THING

You tithe. Attend church faithfully. Sow seeds. Loyal. Honest Trustworthy. Forgive those that aren't even sorry. But you're still going through it. However, the enemy looks as if they're prospering and flourishing. So, now you want to stop. Is that your story?

Don't get fooled and tricked by the enemy and stop. God isn't mocked. What you sow you, shall reap. (Galatians 6:7) And you will reap every righteous act that you've done. (2 Corinthians 9:6)

God isn't blind. He sees all and hears all. (Hebrews 4:13) And He is for YOU!!!!! (Psalm 105:15)

Remember, it is easy to hate, and it is difficult to love. This is how the whole scheme of things works. All good things are difficult to achieve; and bad things are very easy to get. (Confucius)

"He who trusts in his riches will fall, But the righteous will flourish like the green leaf." (Proverbs 11:28)

In fact, it is easier for a camel to go through the eye of a needle than for a rich person to enter the Kingdom of God!" (Mark 10:25)

DO THE RIGHT THING!!!!!!!!!!!

_____
_____
_____
_____
_____
_____

AUGUST 28

BEING ELIMINATED

The slap in the face. The brush off. The job falling through and the relationship ending abruptly. That type of disappointment doesn't feel good at all. In fact, it hurts.

However, you can't t focus so much on the dismissal. Instead, realize that God is blocking you from what you couldn't see. (Psalm 121:7-8)

Always remember this: Closed doors. Rejections. They do not decide your fate. They simply redirect your course. You must keep moving because life's detours can also be meaningful. (Dodinsky)

"And we know that in all things God works for the good of those who love Him, who have been called according to His purpose." (Romans 8:28)

_____
_____
_____
_____
_____
_____
_____
_____
_____
_____
_____
_____

AUGUST 29

YOU'RE SOMEBODY'S ANSWERED PRAYERS

They left you. You got fired. They turned their backs on you. Now you've got a wall up because you don't trust. Does that ring a bell?

Truth is "they" did you a favor. What they thought would break and destroy you. God means for your good. (Genesis 50:20)

So, be glad that they left or let you go. Because God has BETTER in store!!!!!! (Jeremiah 29:11)

Remember, they said no and bye. So, you say THANK YOU!!!! For God is protecting you from less to His best!!!!!

"As you come to him, the living stone who was rejected by people but was chosen and precious in God's sight," (1 Peter 2:4)

AUGUST 30

THIS STRESS IS KILLING ME

Stress. Who hasn't had that in their lives? Being stressed is a state of mental or emotional strain or tension resulting from adverse or very demanding circumstances.

YES! You have every right to be stressed out and overwhelmed by the circumstances that have succumbed you. But does that mean that you crawl up and die? NO! It means that you fight and declare and decree your situation fixed, healed and resolved. Speak as if it is done. (Proverbs 18:21)

Remember, if you are distressed by anything external, the pain is not due to the thing itself, but to your estimate of it; and this you have the power to revoke at any moment." (Marcus Aurelius)

"Truly, I say to you, whoever says to this mountain, 'Be taken up and thrown into the sea,' and does not doubt in his heart, but believes that what he says will come to pass, it will be done for him." (Mark 11:23)

AUGUST 31

ACT LIKE YOU CAN'T FAIL

You want to do it, but you're scared. Even though you know God doesn't give you the spirit of fear. (2 Timothy 1:7) However, you still don't want to make the leap of faith.

Instead of worrying about the failures of trying and the what ifs, see yourself as if you have conquered your biggest fear. And living the best days of your life from the desires of your heart. (Psalm 37:4)

Just think, what would you attempt if you knew you could not fail? (Robert H. Schuller)

"I can do all things through Him who strengthens me." (Philippians 4:13)

SEPTEMBER 1

THE BEST REVENGE

Plotting. Scheming. Concocting. Conspiring. That's what you do when you're secretly making plans to carry out on someone that has done you wrong. Now, that isn't you, is it?

It's understandable why you want to get revenge and do to them what they've done to you. But you can't. God says that vengeance is His and He will repay. (Romans 12:19) YOU just need to be still and watch the deliverance of the Lord. (Exodus 14:13)

Remember, the best revenge is to be unlike him who performed the injury. (Marcus Aurelius)

"But I tell you, love your enemies and pray for those who persecute you, that you may be children of your Father in heaven. He causes his sun to rise on the evil and the good and sends rain on the righteous and the unrighteous." (Matthew 5:44-45)

SEPTEMBER 2

ROCK YOU

Intimation and duplicating are what the world does now. Once a person see's someone else with it or do it...they must have it and do it too. But what's wrong with, being YOU?

There comes a time that replicating must cease and desist. But setting the stage and standard should start with YOU!!!

Remember, to be yourself in a world that is constantly trying to make you something else is the greatest accomplishment. (Ralph Waldo Emerson)

"For we are God's handiwork, created in Christ Jesus to do good works, which God prepared in advance for us to do." (Ephesians 2:10)

SEPTEMBER 3

THE ECHOES IN ETERNITY

I'll change tomorrow. I still have time. God knows my heart. That's not you, is it?

Fact is tomorrow is not promised. (James 4:13-14) You think that you can wait and get your life right later. However, what if you keep putting off what you should do today for tomorrow, but tomorrow doesn't come?

It's time to stop playing!!!!!

Remember, what we do now echoes in eternity. (Marcus Aurelius)

"Do not boast about tomorrow, For you do not know what a day may bring forth." (Proverbs 27:1)

SEPTEMBER 4

SEEING YOURSELF

I need to lose weight. My hair is awful. I hate my skin. My curves are hideous. Now, that isn't you putting yourself down, is it?

Fact is, no matter how you see yourself. You must know that you are fearfully and wonderfully made. (Psalm 139:14) There comes a time that you have to stop comparing yourself to what you think you should look like. And thank God for how beautiful and handsome He has made you. (1 Peter 3:3-4)

Remember, learn to see yourself as Heavenly Father sees you - as His precious daughter or son with divine potential. (Dieter F. Uchtdorf)

"You are altogether beautiful, my love; there is no flaw in you." (Song of Solomon 4:7)

SEPTEMBER 5

INTIMIDATED & TERRORIZED, BUT SURVIVED

How many of you know what it feels like to be attacked? Whether it was from the North, South, East or West. You're a living testimony that what he meant for evil God means for your good. (Genesis 50:20)

Fact is you're a survivor and made for the struggle. So, before you fall out or crawl up in the bed because you're sick and tired of being sick and tired. Count it all joy. (James 1:2)

Because the enemy thought he would take you out. But just go look in the mirror. If you see yourself that means that you're still alive. (A SURVIVOR)

Remember, you can't be intimidated when you've already been terrorized and survived!!!! (Pastor Jamal Bryant)

"They triumphed over him by the blood of the Lamb and by the word of their testimony;" (Revelation 12:11)

_____
_____
_____
_____
_____
_____
_____
_____
_____

SEPTEMBER 6

YOU'RE NOT SINKING

2017 hasn't come to an end yet. And all you're thinking about is how you're ready for 2018 because this has been the worst year of your life. Sound familiar?

The divorce. The breakup. The losses. They're all too much to bear. But you need to cry later and shout NOW. For weeping may endure for a moment but joy does come in the morning. (Psalm 30:5)

God doesn't take anything away without replacing it with something better.

Remember, we should feel sorrow, but not sink under its oppression. (Confucius)

"We are pressed on every side by troubles, but we are not crushed. We are perplexed, but not driven to despair." (2 Corinthians 4:8)

SEPTEMBER 7

THE STRENGTH FOR IT

You don't know how you're going to get it done. You don't know where the money is going to come from. You're mentally and physically tired because it's too much to bear. Sound familiar?

Fact is God is with YOU!!! And you have the strength to endure the struggle. (Isaiah 41:10) You might feel tired and weak. But God gives strength to the weary and increases the power of the weak. (Isaiah 40:29)

Remember, at times, our strengths propel us so far forward we can no longer endure our weaknesses and perish from them. (Friedrich Nietzsche)

"That is why, for Christ's sake, I delight in weaknesses, in insults, in hardships, in persecutions, in difficulties. For when I am weak, then I am strong." (2 Corinthians 12:10)

SEPTEMBER 8

COUNTING THE BLESSINGS OR PROBLEMS

Have you ever been in a car wreck and were more upset about the car than the fact you could have been killed in the wreck?

In life sometimes, we focused more on the problems that have occurred, rather than the blessings that are upon us.

Remember, better to lose count while naming your blessings than to lose your blessings to counting your troubles. (Maltbie D. Babcock)

"Rejoice always, pray without ceasing, give thanks in all circumstances; for this is the will of God in Christ Jesus for you." (1 Thessalonians 5:16-18)

SEPTEMBER 9

START MAKING SOME ADJUSTMENTS

You think you can't do it. They said you can't. It looks like you're out of money. You don't know what else to do. Before you have a panic attack, ask yourself, do you trust man or God?

Just because the possible seems impossible doesn't mean that you should give up. Fact is what is impossible with man is possible with God. (Luke 18:27)

Remember, when it is obvious that the goals cannot be reached, don't adjust the goals, adjust the action steps. (Confucius)

So, start walking by faith and not by sight! (2 Corinthians 5:7)

"For nothing is impossible with God.'" (Luke 1:37)

SEPTEMBER 10

BUT I WANT SOMETHING BETTER

I need a bigger house. I need a better car. I need a new man. I need to get a better wife. Now that isn't you, is it?

You've heard the saying before, the grass isn't always greener on the other side. Truth be told, it's not. Sometimes you might find out that the grass is a bunch of brown weeds instead. Nothing that you expected at all.

It's a foolish person that wants to replace God's blessings with something else. (2 Timothy 3:1-5)

Remember, he is a wise man who does not grieve for the things which he has not, but rejoices for which he has. (Epictetus)

"I know what it is to be in need, and I know what it is to have plenty. I have learned the secret of being content in any and every situation, whether well-fed or hungry, whether living in plenty or in want." (Philippians 4:12)

SEPTEMBER 11

GETTING COMFORTABLE IN THE UNCOMFORTABLE

Things might not be what you want right now. But it could be worse. How many of you can relate?

See, God is doing something new in your life. (Isaiah 43:19) And it will cause you to be uncomfortable for a moment. But in the end, it will be worth it.

Remember, whatever makes you uncomfortable is your biggest opportunity for growth. (Bryant McGill)

"Blessed be the God and Father of our Lord Jesus Christ, the Father of mercies and God of all comfort, who comforts us in all our affliction, so that we may be able to comfort those who are in any affliction, with the comfort with which we ourselves are comforted by God." (2 Corinthians 1:3-4)

_____
_____
_____
_____
_____
_____
_____
_____
_____
_____
_____
_____

SEPTEMBER 12

STOP ARGUING WITH THEM

He should have done this. She did the wrong thing. They had no right doing that. Can you relate?

Truth is there is always going to be someone or something that isn't going to sit well with you. But that doesn't mean that you have to argue and act a fool with them.

Remember, waste no more time arguing about what a good man should be. Be one. (Marcus Aurelius)

"Don't have anything to do with foolish and stupid arguments, because you know they produce quarrels." (2 Timothy 2:23)

SEPTEMBER 13

STOP LETTING THEM GET TO YOU

Some folks can be just low down, mean and hateful. But does that mean that you should stoop down to their level? NO!

Former First Lady Michelle Obama once said, "When they go low we go high." But when they go low we should go to our knees in prayer and pray for those that mistreat and misuse us. (Luke 6:28)

At the end of the day, what you can do is one thing. But what God can do to your enemies is another. (Romans 12:19)

Remember, do not let the behavior of others destroy your inner peace. (Dalai Lama)

"I will take revenge; I will pay them back. In due time, their feet will slip. Their day of disaster will arrive, and their destiny will overtake them.' "Indeed, the LORD will give justice to his people," (Deuteronomy 32:35-36)

SEPTEMBER 14

BUT WHAT DO YOU SEE

In this life, storms are going to blow your way that are going to be out of your control. Does it look bad? YES! But what does God say?

God says for you to put your trust in Him and not in man. (Psalm 118:8) For we live by Faith and not by sight. (2 Corinthians 5:7) No matter what "they" said or how bad it looks. See yourself out of the storm and everything working together for your good. (Romans 8:28)

Remember, it's not what you look at that matters, it's what you see. (Henry David Thoreau)

"So, we fix our eyes not on what is seen, but on what is unseen. For what is seen is temporary, but what is unseen is eternal." (2 Corinthians 4:18)

SEPTEMBER 15

IT'S TIME TO GET DIRTY

Life can be fair and unfair. For God causes the sun to rise on the Just and Unjust. (Matthew 5:45) Does that mean you crawl up and roll over? NO!

But it does mean that you get dirty and fight the good fight of faith. (1 Timothy 6:12) YES, it's not right and it looks bad. But God won't let your enemies and this situation succumb you. (Psalm 121:7) Put your trust in God and not in man and watch the salvation on the Lord on your behalf. (2 Chronicles 20:17)

Remember, to survive it is often necessary to fight and to fight you have to dirty yourself. (George Orwell)

"I have fought the good fight, I have finished the race, I have kept the faith." (2 Timothy 4:7)

SEPTEMBER 16

ACT LIKE YOU HAVE RISEN

There will come a time in everyone's life where they will fall. The question is, do you stay down when you've fallen?

No matter what has taken place in your life. You must make the decision to get back up after the calamity strikes. YES, it hurts and it's bad. But you're not going to stay there. (1 Corinthians 10:13)

Remember, every man is free to rise as far as he's able or willing, but the degree to which he thinks determines the degree to which he'll rise. (Ayn Rand)

"For the righteous falls seven times and rises again," (Proverbs 24:16)

SEPTEMBER 17

I'M DROWNING

Have you ever felt like you were drowning by the adversity of life? More bills than money. Job stress. Church woes. Relationship heartbreak and family trouble. Sound familiar?

With that much hardship and calamity at once, it can be extremely overwhelming. But thank God, we know that troubles don't last always. (2 Corinthians 4:17) God is with us through it all. (Joshua 1:9)

Remember, you don't drown by falling in the water; you drown by staying there. (Edwin Louis Cole)

"When you pass through the waters, I will be with you; and when you pass through the rivers, they will not sweep over you. When you walk through the fire, you will not be burned; the flames will not set you ablaze." (Isaiah 43:2)

SEPTEMBER 18

SIGNALING FOR HELP

Let me call my girlfriend to help me out. I need to get the fellas together and talk about this. I hope my mom and dad are there to help me. Sound familiar?

When you're in a desperate state of needing help it can be overwhelming. Not knowing who to call or what to do can cause unnecessary chaos.

But before you call any and everybody. You must first call on The Lord. (Psalm 145:18)

Remember, the faster you can signal for rescue, the faster you get out of that situation. (Joseph Teti)

"Then call on me when you are in trouble, and I will rescue you, and you will give me glory."' (Psalm 50:15)

_____
_____
_____
_____
_____
_____
_____
_____
_____
_____
_____

SEPTEMBER 19

I DON'T LOOK LIKE WHAT I'VE BEEN THROUGH

I don't look like what I've been through!!!! How many of you have that statement as your testimony?

See, your character is your mental and moral qualities. This is what you're made up of. And everything that you've been through has made you stronger and wiser today.

Remember, character cannot be developed in ease and quiet. Only through experience of trial and suffering can the soul be strengthened, ambition inspired, and success achieved. (Helen Keller)

"More than that, we rejoice in our sufferings, knowing that suffering produces endurance, and endurance produces character, and character produces hope, and hope does not put us to shame, because God's love has been poured into our hearts through the Holy Spirit who has been given to us." (Romans 5:3-5)

_____
_____
_____
_____
_____
_____
_____
_____
_____

SEPTEMBER 20

WHO IS WRITING YOUR SCRIPT

You can't do this. I don't want you. You will never make it. Has anyone ever told you that?

Fact is "they" can say what they will and won't do. But can't nobody take the promises away from you that God has for your life. (Jeremiah 29:11)

So, stop letting a NO stop your show.

Remember, YOU define your own life. Don't let other people write your script. (Oprah Winfrey)

Jesus looked at them and said, "With man this is impossible, but with God all things are possible."" (Matthew 19:26)

SEPTEMBER 21

THE WORRY OF TODAY, YESTERDAY & TOMORROW

Worry is to give way to anxiety or unease; allow one's mind to dwell on difficulty or troubles. Now, that isn't you, is it?

Fact is God doesn't give us a spirit of fear. (2 Timothy 1:7) You have nothing to upset yourself over. Every worry and care that you have must be turned over to the Lord. (1 Peter 5:7)

Truth be told....It's already handled!!! (Romans 8:28)

Remember, today is the tomorrow you worried about yesterday. (Dale Carnegie)

The Lord replied, "you are worried and upset about many things." (Luke 10:41) "Can all your worries add a single moment to your life?" (Matthew 6:27)

SEPTEMBER 22

ACCEPT THE LOSS

Everybody wants to be a winner, and nobody wants to lose. However, losing isn't as bad as you think. And sometimes, it's necessary.

So, stop crying over your loss. You probably can't see it yet, but there is a lesson in every loss.

Remember, sometimes you win, sometimes you learn. (John C. Maxwell)

"Stand firm, and you will win life." (Luke 21:19)

SEPTEMBER 23

STOP GOING BACK ON YOUR WORD

You told them that you were going to do it. But you didn't show up. You made a promise. But didn't keep it. Now, that wouldn't be you, is it?

Stop going back on your word. That is what you have. If you make a promise, oath or vow, stick to it. (Numbers 30:2)

Remember, your thoughts should agree with your words, and the words should agree with your actions. In this world people think one thing, say another thing, and do something else. This is horrible. This is crookedness. (Swami Sivananda)

""Again, you have heard that it was said to the people long ago, 'Do not break your oath, but fulfill to the Lord the vows you have made.'" (Matthew 5:33)

SEPTEMBER 24

THE TWO THIEVES IN YOUR LIFE

I should have done it differently. What if it doesn't work out? If Only.... The wouldas, couldas and shouldas in life can drive you crazy.

Fact is God doesn't give us a spirit of fear. (2 Timothy 1:7) There is no reason that you should be afraid to walk into your future. And it's time for you to release the things of the past. (Isaiah 43:18)

YES, it didn't work out the way YOU thought. Truth is it worked out EXACTLY in your favor. You probably just haven't seen it yet. But keep on living!!!!

Remember, many of us crucify ourselves between two thieves - regret for the past and fear of the future. (Fulton Oursler)

"So, don't be afraid, little flock. For it gives your Father great happiness to give you the Kingdom." (Luke 12:32)

SEPTEMBER 25

STOP WATCHING THE CLOCK

Sitting on the job waiting for 5:00 o'clock to hit. At the doctor's office, constantly looking at your watch wondering how long it's been since you've been sitting there. Sound familiar?

Unfortunately, we live in a world that we can have everything RIGHT NOW. But that's not reality. Sometimes what you want is going to require you to wait and have patience. So, stop watching the clock and do what it does and keep on going.

Remember, the two most powerful warriors are patience and time. (Leo Tolstoy)

"But if we hope for what we do not see, we wait for it with patience." (Romans 8:25)

SEPTEMBER 26

KEEP BEING IGNORANT OR BE WISE

Folks can be mean, ugly and nasty in their ways. But just because you're sweet, nice and loving doesn't mean that they're going to be like that as well.

You can't treat folks like they treat you, no matter how low they go. YES, there might be an instance where you want to go off, pop off and set it off on them. But you can't do that.

Don't fall for the trap of the ignorant devices of the enemy. (Ephesians 6:11) You're better than that!

Remember, not engaging in ignorance is wisdom. (Bodhidharma)

"Whoever restrains his words has knowledge, and he who has a cool spirit is a man of understanding. Even a fool who keeps silent is considered wise; when he closes his lips, he is deemed intelligent." (Proverbs 17:27-28)

SEPTEMBER 27

I NEED

I need to get this done. But I have to get this too. I also need that. Sound familiar? A life full of "NEEDS".

When you're in need of any and everything and don't know what you're going to do to get it. You go to the source, God. (Psalm 16:5)

Remember, everything you need God already is. (Priscilla Shirer)

"And my God will meet all your needs according to the riches of His glory in Christ Jesus." (Philippians 4:19)

SEPTEMBER 28

WHAT'S THE EXCUSE NOW

YOU know you're supposed to start that book. YOU know you should be eating healthier. YOU know that business should be open. So, what's the excuse now?

Fact is, there is so much that you should be doing. But you keep putting off what you should do today for tomorrow. (Proverbs 13:4)

TODAY is HERE!!!! Stop with the excuses and move forward with the gift that God has placed in you to share with others. (1 Peter 4:10)

Remember, the best excuse is to have none. (Ivan Panin)

"Therefore, you have no excuse," (Romans 2:1)

_____
_____
_____
_____
_____
_____
_____
_____
_____
_____
_____
_____
_____

SEPTEMBER 29

WHAT ARE YOU GOING TO SAY?

We live in a world now that you can say what you want to say. There is Facebook allowing you to go LIVE. Instagram. Snapchat and Twitter. Where you can reach thousands of people daily all waiting to hear what you are going to say.

So, what are you going to say? Is it positive or negative? Words should be gracious like honeycomb. Sweetness to the soul and health to the body. (Proverbs 16:24)

Remember, be Impeccable with Your Word. Speak with integrity. Say only what you mean. Avoid using the word to speak against yourself or to gossip about others. Use the power of your word in the direction of truth and love. (Don Miguel Ruiz)

"I tell you, on the day of judgment people will give account for every careless word they speak," (Matthew 12:36)

_____
_____
_____
_____
_____
_____
_____
_____
_____

SEPTEMBER 30

DON'T WORRY, IT WILL COME BACK

A loss can be hard to take. Whether it's a loss of a person, material possession, or even a job. But everything you lose isn't a loss.

Sometimes God must slam, close and shut a door on you because you can't do it yourself. You are weeping over something that God is about to give you double for.

If you knew what BLESSING(S) was coming to you because you let go of the loss would you still be weeping?

Remember, don't grieve. Anything you lose comes around in another form. (Rumi)

"Instead of your shame you will receive a double portion, and instead of disgrace you will rejoice in your inheritance. And so you will inherit a double portion in your land, and everlasting joy will be yours. (Isaiah 61:7)

OCTOBER 1

ARE YOU CORRECTING OR ENCOURAGING

Just stop, let me do it. You're doing it wrong. Well, go ahead and do it then. But secretly inside you want them to fail. Now, is that you?

Correcting is telling someone that they're mistaken. Encouraging is when you give someone support in being positive and hope in their future endeavor and or promise. There is a difference between correcting and encouraging. Which are you?

Remember, correction does much, but encouragement does more. (Johann Wolfgang Von Goethe)

"Let no corrupting talk come out of your mouths, but only such as is good for building up, as fits the occasion, that it may give grace to those who hear." (Ephesians 4:29)

OCTOBER 2

THE AUTHORITY IN YOUR SILENCE

When you're under attack it seems like everywhere you turn you're getting hit by a shot. At Home. Work. Church. Relationships and Finances.

The easy thing to do is to lash out. But that makes you more frustrated. You cry and pray. Pray and cry. But still nothing.

So, now you must be still and let the Lord fight your battle. (Exodus 14:14)

Remember, nothing strengthens authority so much as silence. (Leonardo da Vinci)

"My soul, wait in silence for God only, for my hope is from Him." (Psalm 62:5)

OCTOBER 3

MY HERO

When people think about heroes they think of a person admired for their achievements, courage and strength. Normally, they are quick to name someone that they look up too. But have you ever thought about everything that you've come through?

Fact is YOU are a hero. YOU are still standing with all the fiery darts, shots and knives that were thrown at. The enemy tried his best shot to take you out and down. But look at you now.

Remember, a hero is an ordinary individual who finds the strength to persevere and endure in spite of overwhelming obstacles. (Christopher Reeve)

"Greatly have they afflicted me from my youth, yet they have not prevailed against me." (Psalm 129:2)

_____
_____
_____
_____
_____
_____
_____
_____
_____
_____
_____
_____

OCTOBER 4

YOU WAS TAUGHT BETTER THAN THAT

No Mam. Yes Sir. Thank you and You're Welcome. Those are all things that we learned at an early age on how to talk to people and what to do and what not to do.

So, if life is like a roller coaster for you right now. And you KNOW that you need to walk by faith and not by sight. (2 Corinthians 5:7) Why aren't you doing it?

Remember, knowing is not enough; we must apply. Willing is not enough; we must do. (Johann Wolfgang von Goethe)

""Truly I tell you," Jesus replied, "if you have faith and do not doubt, not only will you do what was done to the fig tree, but even if you say to this mountain, 'Be lifted up and thrown into the sea,' it will happen." (Matthew 21:21)

OCTOBER 5

THANK YOU FOR THE EXPERIENCE

Have you ever been done so wrong that it has left you bitter, scorned and hurt? Truth be told you're so messed up now you don't even trust at all. What type of life is that to have?

It's time to release all that hurt, anger, rage and resentment that you have. (Ephesians 4:31) God wants to take you to another level but He can't because you're holding on to the person that has wronged you yesterday or years ago. Forgive them and LET IT GO!!!

Remember, true forgiveness is when you can say, "Thank you for that experience. **(**Oprah Winfrey)

""But if you do not forgive, neither will your Father who is in heaven forgive your transgressions."" (Mark 11:26)

OCTOBER 6

THE SECRET FOR CHANGING YOUR FUTURE

I can't stand working with her. He gets on my last nerves. Does that sound like you? Is there someone in your life that the mere thought of them makes you sick?

Instead of wishing and wanting them to go away. Change how you deal with them. YES, they might be a jerk. But at the end of the day....YOU are only responsible for your words, actions and attitude.

Remember, the greatest discovery of all time is that a person can change his future by merely changing his attitude. (Oprah Winfrey)

"Say to the righteous that it will go well with them, for they will eat the fruit of their actions." (Isaiah 3:10)

OCTOBER 7

UNNECESSARY SUFFERING

Suffering is the state of undergoing pain, distress, or hardship. Who hasn't been there a time or two? But what do you do when you're there?

Well, you don't need to trip and cause unnecessary stress when trials come your way. Instead, count it all joy and know that the testing of your faith produces steadfastness.   (James 1:2-4)

That's easier said than done. But know that you will get through that suffering. God is good, and He is always there so try to focus on the good that is to come.

Remember, a man who suffers before it is necessary, suffers more than is necessary. (Lucius Annaeus Seneca)

"More than that, we rejoice in our sufferings, knowing that suffering produces endurance, and endurance produces character, and character produces hope, and hope does not put us to shame, because God's love has been poured into our hearts through the Holy Spirit who has been given to us." (Romans 5:3-5)

OCTOBER 8

IS THIS THE END?

Devastated. Ruined. Lost. Broken. Depressed. Do you know what that feels like? Imagine having all those feelings at once.

For some they feel like it's the end of the world. However, you must count it all joy for the sufferings that you endure. (James 1:2) Always rejoice in hope, be patient in tribulation, and be constant in prayer. (Romans 12:12)

Remember, everything will be okay in the end. If it's not okay, it's not the end. (John Lennon)

"Think back on those early days when you first learned about Christ. Remember how you remained faithful even though it meant terrible suffering." (Hebrews 10:32)

"More than that, we rejoice in our sufferings, knowing that suffering produces endurance, and endurance produces character, and character produces hope, and hope does not put us to shame, because God's love has been poured into our hearts through the Holy Spirit who has been given to us." (Romans 5:3-5)

_____
_____
_____
_____
_____
_____

OCTOBER 9

A SUDDEN IMPACT

The definition of impact is a strong effect on someone or something. How many sudden impacts have you had to deal with leaving you speechless and devastated?

It doesn't feel good, does it? So, have you ever thought about the impact that you do to others and the hell that it might cause?

Remember, every action we take impacts the lives of others around us. (Arthur Carmazzi)

Be aware of the impact you're making!!!!

"Be kind to one another, tender-hearted, forgiving each other, just as God in Christ also has forgiven you." (Ephesians 4:32)

OCTOBER 10

REACTING OR DECIDING

Fear is an unpleasant emotion caused by the belief that someone or something is dangerous, likely to cause pain, or a threat. However, God doesn't give us a spirit of fear. (2 Timothy 1:7) But folks are still scared.

It's time to walk in the authority that you have. And you have just that....POWER & AUTHORITY over the enemy. (Luke 10:19) Make the decision now by declaring and decreeing that you WIN. Not even the devil in hell can take what God has promised you. (John 10:10)

Remember, fear is a reaction. Courage is a decision. (Sir Winston Churchill)

"Have I not commanded you? Be strong and courageous. Do not be frightened, and do not be dismayed, for the Lord your God is with you wherever you go.'" (Joshua 1:9)

OCTOBER 11

A RIVER CUTS THROUGH ROCKS

Distressed. Tired. Frustrated. Heartbroken. Weary. Who hasn't felt like that at some point in their life?

Do you give up? NO! But you do continue to press on. (Philippians 3:14) You might not feel like you have the power to continue. BUT YOU DO!!!! Because you are being strengthened with all power according to His glorious might. So, that you may have great endurance and patience to continue the race. (Colossians 1:11)

Remember, a river cuts through rock, not because of its power, but because of its persistence. (James N. Watkins)

YOU GOT THIS!!!!!!!!

"We are pressed on every side by troubles, but we are not crushed. We are perplexed, but not driven to despair. We are hunted down, but never abandoned by God. We get knocked down, but we are not destroyed." (2 Corinthians 4:8-9)

OCTOBER 12

"THE MEMORY" (WAS IT TRUE OR FALSE)

Memories are something remembered from the past as a recollection. We all have them. However, are you remembering exactly the truth, or do you see it the way that you want to see it.

It's easy to get caught up in the way you wanted it to go. But at the end of the day, truth is truth, no matter how you want to see it.

Remember, the difference between false memories and true ones is the same as for jewels: it is always the false ones that look the most real, the most brilliant. (Salvador Dali)

"And you will know the truth, and the truth will set you free."" (John 8:32)

_____
_____
_____
_____
_____
_____
_____
_____
_____
_____
_____
_____

OCTOBER 13

FAILED PLANS NOT FAILED VISIONS

I tried it, but it didn't work. Does that mean your vision is gone? NO!

Please don't get weary in well doing. (Galatians 6:9) Is it hard? YES! Is it worth it? YES!!! Truth is, you must keep going no matter how hard the winds may blow and how hard the rain comes. Your vision will come to pass but you must be patient and wait. (Habakkuk 2:3)

Remember, failed plans should not be interpreted as a failed vision. (John C. Maxwell)

"The Lord isn't really being slow about his promise, as some people think. No, he is being patient for your sake. He does not want anyone to be destroyed, but wants everyone to repent." (2 Peter 3:9)

_____
_____
_____
_____
_____
_____
_____
_____
_____
_____
_____

OCTOBER 14

GOD'S PROMISE OR YOUR WANTS?

Have you ever been in a place where you feel like God has forgotten about you? You pray, fast and stand in prayer but your prayers are still not answered.

Truth is God hasn't forgotten about you. (Isaiah 49:15-16) But you must ask yourself are you praying for the thing that God has told you to let go of? (Isaiah 43:18-19)

Remember, there is a huge difference between believing what God has promised and praying for things you'd like to be true. (Francis Chan)

"I know what I'm doing. I have it all planned out—plans to take care of you, not abandon you, plans to give you the future you hope for." (Jeremiah 29:11) MSG

OCTOBER 15

THE DISTANCE BETWEEN PROBLEMS

The definition of a problem is a matter or situation regarded as unwelcome or harmful needing to be dealt with and overcome. Problems can arise when we least expect them. So, what do you do?

You may have a problem, but it doesn't mean that it's the end of the world. It's not the time to fall out, give up or give in. You must fight! And you do that on your knees in prayer.

We must remember that the shortest distance between our problems and their solutions is the distance between our knees and the floor. (Charles Stanley)

"Then you will call on me and come and pray to me, and I will listen to you." (Jeremiah 29:12)

OCTOBER 16

STOP RUNNING AROUND LIKE A FIREFIGHTER?

A firefighter is a rescuer that is trained extensively in putting out fires. How many of you feel like you are constantly putting out fires daily in your life?

Often the fires that we end up putting out we didn't even start. But have you ever looked at the fires that started that were lit by your own hands?

Remember, some people procrastinate so much that all they can do is run around like firefighters all day - putting out fires that should not have gotten started in the first place. (Nido R Qubein)

"The soul of the sluggard craves and gets nothing, while the soul of the diligent is richly supplied." (Proverbs 13:4)

OCTOBER 17

THINGS ARE MOVING SLOW

Does it seem like the things that you're trying to make happen and do are taking forever to get off the ground? You've done everything right. Prayed. Gone to church. Tithed. Sown seeds. Even encouraged others. But, NOTHING.

Well, what you're not going to do... is give up. Fact is you can never get tired of doing the right and good thing. You will reap your harvest if you don't give up. (Galatians 6:9) YES, it might seem like it is moving slow. But just hold tight a little longer. Your blessing is coming.

Remember, the trees that are slow to grow, bear the best fruit. (Molière)

"Therefore, my dear brothers and sisters, stand firm. Let nothing move you. Always give yourselves fully to the work of the Lord, because you know that your labor in the Lord is not in vain." (1 Corinthians 15:58)

OCTOBER 18

WORK NEVER KILLED ANYONE

Tomorrow is the day I'll do it. I promise I'm going to get it done today. That's not you, is it?

See, it's easy to keep putting off what you need to do TODAY for tomorrow. However, last minute worries and woes, it's not good for the soul.

Remember, work never killed anyone. It's worry that does the damage. And the worry would disappear if we'd just settle down and do the work. (Earl Nightingale)

"Diligent hands will rule, but laziness ends in forced labor." (Proverbs 12:24)

OCTOBER 19

LITTLE HINGES SWING BIG DOORS

Looks can be deceiving. Just because you aren't bawling out of control doesn't mean you don't have what "it" takes to get it done. Stop getting fooled by the hype.

Yes, the bank account might say one thing. And by looking at it with your natural eyes you don't meet the requirements. BUT GOD!!!!!

You must know that God is not like humans that He shall lie. And He doesn't change His mind either. If He has spoken a thing in your life, He will fulfill it!!!!! (Numbers 23:19)

Remember, little hinges swing big doors. (W. Clement Stone)

"So God has given both his promise and his oath. These two things are unchangeable because it is impossible for God to lie. Therefore, we who have fled to Him for refuge can have great confidence as we hold to the hope that lies before us." (Hebrews 6:18)

OCTOBER 20
YOUR SPEED IS INCREASING

Have you ever had a dream where you're trying to go faster but the more you try it seems as if gravity is pulling you back the other way? Sometimes, that's how life can be. You get up only to get knocked, pushed, dragged and thrown down. Al Sharpton says, if you get knocked down that's on them. But a week later if you're still down, that's on YOU!!!!

So, it's time to get up and keep on keeping on. (Philippians 3:14) Truth is you're closer than what you think. That's why the enemy keeps attacking and coming for you. You can't see it, but you're already there and you're about to take off.

Just remember, once you're over the hill you begin to pick up speed. (Arthur Schopenhauer)

"We do this by keeping our eyes on Jesus, the champion who initiates and perfects our faith. Because of the joy awaiting him, he endured the cross, disregarding its shame. Now he is seated in the place of honor beside God's throne." (Hebrews 12:2)

OCTOBER 21

IT'S NOT THE END OF THE WORLD

You might be going through a hard and difficult time right now. It might feel like it's the end of the world. BUT GOD!!!!

See, everything isn't what it appears to be. YES, the divorce is happening. The bank account says $5.00. But God still reigns. (Psalm 47:8)

Remember, what the caterpillar calls the end of the world, the master calls a butterfly. (Richard Bach)

"Therefore I tell you, do not worry about your life, what you will eat or drink; or about your body, what you will wear. Is not life more than food, and the body more than clothes? Look at the birds of the air; they do not sow or reap or store away in barns, and yet your heavenly Father feeds them. Are you not much more valuable than they? (Matthew 6:25-26)

OCTOBER 22

YOUR DREAM IS STILL ALIVE

It seems impossible. Doors keep getting closed. There is no money for you to get it done. So, because of the setbacks you've decided to stop dreaming and give up.

See, that's what the enemy wants you to do. He wants you to think that your hopes and dreams are dead. But thank God, we know that God is a God of resurrection. (Luke 24)

What's in YOU is so big and so powerful that the enemy wants to stop it from getting out. So, he will try every trick and scheme to make you doubt God's promise for your life. (Ephesians 6:10-18) HE'S A LIE!!!!! (John 8:44)

Remember, God didn't make a mistake giving you your dream. You already have enough in you for your dream to come out. (Devon Franklin)

"With man this is impossible, but with God all things are possible." (Matthew 19:26)

OCTOBER 23

A LEARNED FOOL VS. AN IGNORANT FOOL

A person who acts unwisely or imprudently. That's a definition of a fool. Are you acting like a fool?

Truth is everyone has or will act a fool at some point in their life. But are you going to keep acting like that or are you going to grow and learn from your mistakes? (1 Corinthians 13:11)

Remember, a learned fool is more a fool than an ignorant fool. (Molière)

"One who is wise is cautious and turns away from evil, but a fool is reckless and careless." (Proverbs 14:16)

OCTOBER 24

YOU ARE MORE THAN YOUR NAME

Your name is Victoria and you went through a tragic divorce. YES, suicide you THOUGHT was a way out. BUT GOD!!!!

At the end of the day everyone has a Victoria in them. Although, the Victoria might be Victor and the divorce might be molestation. There is an "IT" that you must face and release to get to the greatness that God has called you to be. (Philippians 4:13) & (1 Peter 2:9)

Remember, we know what we are, but know not what we may be. (William Shakespeare)

"No, in all these things we are more than conquerors through him who loved us." (Romans 8:37)

_____
_____
_____
_____
_____
_____
_____
_____
_____
_____
_____
_____

OCTOBER 25

YOU CAN'T HEAR, BECAUSE YOU TALK TOO MUCH

You must have the last word. The conversation you dominate. You've talked so much that you didn't hear a word that was being said. Now, that isn't you, is it?

It's time to come to the realization that you're talking too much. A person that is just talking and talking, can't hear what is being said. How do you know that God didn't tell you the answer to your prayers because you were talking and not being silent and listening?

Remember, listen with the intent to understand, not the intent to reply. (Stephen Covey)

"For God speaks time and again, but a person may not notice it." (Job 33:14)

OCTOBER 26

TRUTH WILL ALWAYS BE TRUTH

Folks are going to talk. Growing up you would hear Saints say, "let them talk." At the end of the day you can't stop folks from talking.

Yes, they might be telling lies and spreading awful gossip about you. But it's not for you to handle. God sees and hears all. He will handle your foes. (Hebrews 4:13)

Remember, truth will always be truth, regardless of lack of understanding, disbelief or ignorance. (W. Clement Stone)

"And you will know the truth, and the truth will set free you."" (John 8:32)

OCTOBER 27

IT'S NOT ABOUT THE SIZE OF THE DOG

Big dogs. Small dogs. Some folks just don't like dogs. However, sometimes it's not about the dog at all. It's about the bark in the dog.

Unfortunately, this message is not even about dogs. But it is about the very thing that YOU are dealing with that you're afraid of facing because the bark has you so afraid that it's going to bite you?

Remember, it's not the size of the dog in the fight, it's the size of the fight in the dog. (Mark Twain)

"For God has not given us the spirit of fear; but of power, and of love, and of a sound mind." (2 Timothy 1:7)

OCTOBER 28

THEIR OPINION IS NOT YOUR REALITY

Everybody has something to say. That's what we call an opinion. A view or judgment formed about something, not necessarily based on fact or knowledge.

Just because folks talk shouldn't affect who you are. They can say what they want to say. At the end of the day, it doesn't take from who God said you are. (1 Peter 2:9)

Remember, don't let someone else's opinion of you become your reality. (Les Brown)

"Obviously, I'm not trying to win the approval of people, but of God. If pleasing people were my goal, I would not be Christ's servant." (Galatians 1:10)

OCTOBER 29

IT SHOULD BE COMMON SENSE

You know better, so you do better. How many times have you heard that? Fact is... it's true!!! So, why don't you?

It should be common sense to know that God can't be mocked. What you sow you shall reap. (Galatians 6:7-8) So, what have you been sowing?

Remember, what is common sense isn't common practice. (Stephen Covey)

"The wicked earns deceptive wages, but he who sows righteousness gets a true reward." (Proverbs 11:18)

OCTOBER 30

ARE YOU LIVING YOUR FEARS OR DREAMS

God doesn't give us a spirit of fear. (2 Timothy 1:7) He just doesn't. There is no place within you that fear should live. So, why does it?

It's time to let go of the worry, concern, doubt and dismay. God has something for you, but He can't give it to you because you are too scared. Let it go!!!

Remember, too many of us are not living our dreams because we are living our fears. (Les Brown)

"Have I not commanded you? Be strong and courageous. Do not be afraid; do not be discouraged, for the LORD your God will be with you wherever you go."" (Joshua 1:9)

OCTOBER 31

IT MUST START WITH YOU

Please leave the situation it's too dangerous for you to continue to stay in it. You really need to continue to stay in the program, it's the best thing for you. Sound familiar? Are you constantly trying to tell someone else what to do and what's best for them?

Unfortunately, you can talk until you are blue in the face. But until they are ready to make the change for themselves. You are going to be talking to yourself.

Remember this motto: Only I can change my life. No one can do it for me. (Carol Burnett)

"A sluggard's appetite is never filled, but the desires of the diligent are fully satisfied." (Proverbs 13:4)

_____
_____
_____
_____
_____
_____
_____
_____
_____
_____

NOVEMBER 1

THE TOOL IN YOUR HAND

Talk is cheap. Have you ever heard that saying before? Truth is you can talk about what you're going to do all day long, but until you put action with it, all you're doing is talking. (James 2:17)

Remember this, a sword never kills anybody; it is a tool in the killer's hand. (Lucius Annaeus Seneca) So what's in your hand?

If you don't know let me tell you. You better praise now and cry later. God has already given you authority over the enemy. YOU WIN!!!!!!!!!! (Luke 10:19)

"Lift up your hands to the holy place and bless the Lord!" (Psalm 134:2)

"For I, the Lord your God, hold your right hand; it is I who say to you, "Fear not, I am the one who helps you."" (Isaiah 41:13)

NOVEMBER 2

THERE IS CONSEQUENCES TO ACTING A FOOL

I'm about to go off. They have one more time to look at me crazy. Is that you? Are you prone to go, pop and set it off quickly?

Truth is there is no need for all that anger. Are they worth you sitting behind bars? Are they worth you being buried 6ft under? NO! So, it's imperative that you cease and desist all that bitterness, rage and anger that sets within. (Ephesians 4:31)

Remember, when anger rises, think of the consequences. (Confucius)

"My dear brothers and sisters, take note of this: Everyone should be quick to listen, slow to speak and slow to become angry, because human anger does not produce the righteousness that God desires." (James 1:19-20)

NOVEMBER 3

DID IT DEFEAT YOU OR DID YOU DEFEAT IT?

Life can be hard. You win some and you lose some. But at the end of the day, you keep fighting the good fight of faith. (1 Timothy 6:12)

So, are you going to throw in the towel because you got knocked down? NO, you're going to get back up and press on.

Remember, when an affliction happens to you, you either let it defeat you, or you defeat it. (Jean-Jacques Rousseau)

"We are hard pressed on every side, but not crushed; perplexed, but not in despair; persecuted, but not abandoned; struck down, but not destroyed." (2 Corinthians 4:8-9)

NOVEMBER 4

IT'S THE FEAR THAT'S KILLING YOU

Worry. Scared. Terrified. Anxious. Nervous. That's a bad combination when put together. But just think, folks are walking around right not suffering from them all.

Truth is why are you worrying? More damage is being done by you worrying than the problem itself. It's time to let it go!!!!

Remember, a man who fears suffering is already suffering from what he fears. (Michel de Montaigne)

"Who of you by worrying can add a single hour to your life?" (Luke 12:25)

NOVEMBER 5

YOU WEREN'T ALWAYS SAVED

Who doesn't have something from their past that they're ashamed of and would be mortified if others knew? Truth be told, you weren't always saved.

Fact is no one is perfect. Everyone has a past. It's called: the good, bad and ugly. And even with all that, God can still use YOU.

Remember, you think your past is a wasteland. But God says He will put a stream through what you've come through to take you to where you're going!!! (Devon Franklin)

"Therefore, if anyone is in Christ, the new creation has come: The old has gone, the new is here! All this is from God, who reconciled us to himself through Christ and gave us the ministry of reconciliation: that God was reconciling the world to himself in Christ, not counting people's sins against them. And he has committed to us the message of reconciliation." (2 Corinthians 5:17-19)

_____
_____
_____
_____
_____
_____
_____
_____
_____

NOVEMBER 6

YOU ACTUALLY WON

Have you ever taken a loss? Losing hurts. Nobody wants to lose. But was it really a loss?

Fact is you have to lose to win sometimes. What you think is devastation, God sees as divine restoration.

Remember, there are some defeats more triumphant than victories. (Michel de Montaigne)

"You intended to harm me, but God intended it all for good." (Genesis 50:20)

NOVEMBER 7

WOULD YOU WANT IT DONE TO YOU?

Have you ever done someone wrong? You knew better but you were so hurt that you wanted them to feel your hurt and pain too.

Truth is an eye for an eye is wrong. (Matthew 5:38-42) You can't take matters like that in your own hands. Yes, it might make you feel good. But what you can do and what the Lord can do are two different things. (Exodus 14:14)

Remember, what you do not want done to yourself, do not do to others. (Confucius)

"Beloved, never avenge yourselves, but leave it to the wrath of God, for it is written, "Vengeance is mine, I will repay, says the Lord."" (Romans 12:19)

_____
_____
_____
_____
_____
_____
_____
_____
_____
_____
_____

NOVEMBER 8

I WANT IT AND I WANT IT NOW

Good things come to those who wait. How many of you have heard that line before? Fact is....it's true!

See, we live in a world that we want everything RIGHT NOW! But we must have patience. There comes a time that you have to quit forcing everything and let God work on His time and not yours.

Remember, our patience will achieve more than our force. (Edmund Burke)

"For still the vision awaits its appointed time; it hastens to the end—it will not lie. If it seems slow, wait for it; it will surely come; it will not delay." (Habakkuk 2:3)

_____
_____
_____
_____
_____
_____
_____
_____
_____
_____
_____
_____
_____
_____

NOVEMBER 9

YOU REALLY DIDN'T LOSE

I can't do it today. I'm sorry I decided to go with someone else. You aren't who I'm looking for. OUCH! Those words don't feel good at all. BUT GOD!!!

Here's the thing. YES, when it looks like you've lost, or you got rejected, it hurts. But count it all joy because God has greater and better in store. (James 1:2)

Remember, if you learn from defeat, you haven't really lost. (Zig Ziglar)

"Blessed is the man who remains steadfast under trial, for when he has stood the test he will receive the crown of life, which God has promised to those who love Him." (James 1:12)

NOVEMBER 10

IT'S DISRUPTING YOUR PRESENT

Have you ever had something bad happened to you that you wish you could forget it? But every time you turn around you keep bringing it up.

It's time to move and get on. Truth is it's the past. It's OVER!!!!!

Remember, forgetting means to stop reliving it. Stop proclaiming it. Stop reliving your past. It's disrupting your present and your future. (Devon Franklin)

""Forget the former things; do not dwell on the past." (Isaiah 43:18)

NOVEMBER 11

IT LIES WITHIN YOU

YES, you see it in front of you. It's been behind you. And yet, you still don't know what to do.

Fact is, you're tripping for no reason. Every struggle and obstacle that you're facing, God has given you the authority to trample and defeat it. (Luke 10:19) Truth is you already won!!!!

Remember, what lies behind us and what lies before us are tiny matters compared to what lies within us. (Ralph Waldo Emerson)

"You, dear children, are from God and have overcome them, because the one who is in you is greater than the one who is in the world." (1 John 4:4)

NOVEMBER 12

WHO SAID SOMETHING IS WRONG WITH YOU?

I don't want you. We are going with someone else. You're not who we're looking for and you're not who we want. OUCH!!!

Now, hearing words like that can hurt to the core. But God!! Truth is "they" aren't hurting you at all. Because what they meant for evil, God means for your good. (Genesis 50:20)

Remember, rejection isn't a sign that something is wrong WITH you, it's a sign that they're wrong FOR you.

"As you come to Him, the living stone, rejected by men, but chosen and precious in God's sight." (1 Peter 2:4)

Thank God For Rejection!!!!

NOVEMBER 13

WATCH WHAT YOU PLANT

What happens when you plant a seed from a vegetable? It sprouts, right?

Well, what do you think happens when you are constantly throwing bad seeds on the ground? Those sprout, too. So, be careful of the seeds that you plant.

Remember, if we don't plant the right things, we will reap the wrong things. It goes without saying. (Maya Angelou)

"'Plant the good seeds of righteousness, and you will harvest a crop of love. Plow up the hard ground of your hearts, for now is the time to seek the LORD, that He may come and shower righteousness upon you.'" (Hosea 10:12)

_____
_____
_____
_____
_____
_____
_____
_____
_____
_____
_____
_____

NOVEMBER 14

I'M BROKE AND POOR

Have you ever felt like you have more bills than money? And when you do get paid it comes and it goes. Making you feel broke.

Unfortunately, that is how a lot of people feel. They think because the bank account says $5.13 that's all they have. BUT GOD says, He will give YOU hidden treasures, riches stored up in secret places. So, that you may know that He is LORD, the one who calls YOU by name. (Isaiah 45:3) You're NOT broke!!!!

Remember, poor is a state of mind. Broke is a place you're just passing through. (Dave Ramsey)

"The blessing of the LORD makes a person rich, and he adds no sorrow with it." (Proverbs 10:22)

NOVEMBER 15

THEY'RE ACTING A COMPLETE FOOL

Have you ever noticed that someone was acting a complete jerk? I mean they were just downright rude and nasty. But you're so quick to talk about them and put them down that you can't see what the root of the problem is.

Instead of ridiculing and talking about folks, why don't you try to pray for them? Truth is you really don't know what they're going through and why they're acting the way they are. So, stop!

Remember, every obnoxious act is a cry for help. (Zig Ziglar)

"Don't look out only for your own interests, but take an interest in others, too." (Philippians 2:4)

NOVEMBER 16

IT'S ONLY IMPOSSIBLE FOR A FOOL

I don't think that's going to work. You probably need to rethink that. That really doesn't sound like a good idea. Do you know someone like that? Always putting the negative talk in your ear?

Truth is only fools listen to folly. (Proverbs 18:13) Because God says all things are possible to those who believe. (Mark 9:23) So, remove the fools in your life and keep pressing toward the mark of the prize. (Philippians 3:14)

Remember, impossible is a word to be found only in the dictionary of fools. (Napoleon Bonaparte)

And you're not a fool!!!!

"Jesus looked at them and said, "With man this is impossible, but with God all things are possible."" (Matthew 19:26)

NOVEMBER 17

STOP THE MADNESS

YES, your boss is wrong. YES, the church folks are hypocrites. YES, you have fake friends. YES, your family is low down. BUT GOD!!!!!

Fact is... life for you ain't no crystal stair. But you're still standing. With every single missile thrown at you, God still blocks the fiery darts. (Psalm 121:7) So, there is no need to complain...God has YOU!!!!!!

Remember, when you complain, you make yourself a victim. Leave the situation, change the situation or accept it. All else is madness. (Eckhart Tolle)

"Not that I am speaking of being in need, for I have learned in whatever situation I am to be content. I know how to be brought low, and I know how to abound. In any and every circumstance, I have learned the secret of facing plenty and hunger, abundance and need." (Philippians 4:11-12)

NOVEMBER 18

THERE IS ONLY ONE-WAY AROUND

Life can be hard. You get up. Only to get knocked down, thrown down and kicked down. But you won't stay down.

YES, are there days that you just want to give up and throw in the towel? You might, but you haven't. Fact is you can't get weary in well-doing. Because you will reap your harvest if you faint not. (Galatians 6:9)

Remember, the only way around is through. (Robert Frost)

"When you go through deep waters, I will be with you. When you go through rivers of difficulty, you will not drown. When you walk through the fire of oppression, you will not be burned up; the flames will not consume you. For I am the LORD, your God, the Holy One of Israel, your Savior." (Isaiah 43:2-3)

NOVEMBER 19

WHO SAID IT'S WRONG?

You can't wear white after Labor Day. Heels with Leggings are wrong. Men can't wear pink. Have you ever heard that before?

The question to ask, who is "they" that said it was wrong? Better yet, what is the standard to say it's wrong?

Remember, wrong does not cease to be wrong because the majority share in it. (Leo Tolstoy)

"Therefore, there is now no condemnation for those who are in Christ Jesus." (Romans 8:1)

NOVEMBER 20

WHAT IF THEY KNEW?

What if they knew I was being abused daily? What if they knew I was being beaten every night? What if they knew I was being molested every morning? What if they knew I tried several ways daily to commit suicide? What if they knew I threw up after every meal? IF they knew, would they still treat me like this? So, would you?

Fact is you don't know what someone is going through. YES, their ways might be low down and nasty. But you can't get down to their level. YOU must pray for them. (Luke 6:28)

Remember, please don't judge people. You don't know what it took for someone to get out of bed, look and feel as presentable as possible and face the day. You never truly know the daily struggles of others. (Karen Salmansohn)

""Do not judge others, and you will not be judged. Do not condemn others, or it will all come back against you. Forgive others, and you will be forgiven." (Luke 6:37)

NOVEMBER 21

DEFENDING A LIE

A lie can hurt to the core. Especially, if you have no way of defending and proving that you're telling the truth.

So, what do you do? Remain still and let the Lord fight on your behalf. (Exodus 14:14) YES, it's easier said than done. However, truthful lips endure forever, but a lying tongue and lies are soon exposed. (Proverbs 12:19)

Remember, a truth can walk naked...but a lie always needs to be dressed. (Khalil Gibran)

"And you will know the truth, and the truth will set you free." (John 8:32)

NOVEMBER 22

THE SITUATION

Everybody has a situation that they deal with. Some good, bad and ugly.

So, how do you deal with it? You don't get defined by what you're going through. Your name is Keisha NOT the divorce that you're enduring.

Remember, meanings are not determined by situations, but we determine ourselves by the meanings we give our situations. (Alfred Adler)

"I have told you these things, so that in me you may have peace. In this world you will have trouble. But take heart! I have overcome the world." (John 16:33)

NOVEMBER 23

SELECTIVE KINDNESS

I ain't speaking to her because she is too stuck up. Man, he thinks he is all that, so I'm not saying nothing to him. They want to be like Joneses, forget them.   Now that isn't you, is it?

See, that attitude right there is ugly, rude and uncalled for. You must let that type of anger, bitterness and malice behavior be put away from you. Fact is, God wants you to be kind to one another and forgiving, as God in Christ forgave you. (Ephesians 4:31-32)

Remember, don't practice "selective kindness," show kindness even to those who don't return it. This is putting our faith in to action. (Dave Willis)

"So, put away all malice and all deceit and hypocrisy and envy and all slander." (1 Peter 2:1)

NOVEMBER 24

YOU DON'T OWE AN EXPLANATION

Have you been wrestling with the thought of leaving or staying? And when you think you've come to a conclusion; the enemy tricks you all over again. (Ephesians 6:10-18)

There comes a time in your life that you must do what is best for YOU. God doesn't want you to stay anywhere that is hurting you. (Lamentations 3:33)

Remember, you are allowed to terminate toxic relationships. You are allowed to walk away from people who hurt you. You don't owe anyone an explanation for taking care of yourself. (Steve Maraboli)

"Do what is good and right in the LORD's sight so it may go well with you. Then you'll enter and possess the good land that the LORD your God promised to your ancestors." (Deuteronomy 6:18)

_____

_____

_____

_____

_____

_____

_____

_____

_____

_____

NOVEMBER 25

START DIGGING TWO GRAVES

Revenge, the action of inflicting hurt or harm on someone for an injury or wrong suffered at their hands. How many of you want to lay hands on someone right now?

Do they deserve it? Probably. Is it right? No. But you must know that God is going to handle it way better than what you or I can. (Exodus 14:14)

Remember, before you embark on a journey of revenge, dig two graves. (Confucius)

"Do not be deceived: God is not mocked, for whatever one sows, that will he also reap." (Galatians 6:7)

_____

_____

_____

_____

_____

_____

_____

_____

_____

_____

_____

_____

NOVEMBER 26

I HATE MY PAST

When folks start thinking about the past it can go a couple of different ways. Sad, happy, mad, angry or hurt.

Truth is the past is just that, it's the past. What happened back then doesn't define you. It's time to leave what's behind and look forward to what's ahead. (Philippians 3:13)

Remember, some of the best lessons are learned from past mistakes. The error of the past is the wisdom of the future. (Dale Turner)

""Forget the former things; do not dwell on the past." (Isaiah 43:18)

"I Hate My Past."

When folks start thinking about the past it can go a couple of different ways. Sad, happy, mad, angry or hurt.

_____
_____
_____
_____
_____
_____
_____
_____
_____
_____
_____
_____

NOVEMBER 27

IF YOUR SCARS COULD TALK

Scars are marks left on the skin or within body tissue where a wound, burn, or sore has not healed completely. But how many of you have scars that are not shown?

Have you ever wondered the story that would be told if your scars could talk? Truth is, the scars say, although the devil thought that he had you, God kept you!!!

Remember, out of suffering have emerged the strongest souls. The most massive characters are seared with scars. (Khalil Gibran)

"He heals the brokenhearted and binds up their wounds." (Psalm 147:3)

NOVEMBER 28

YOU DON'T NEED ANYONE'S PERMISSION

Do you think this is okay? Should I move forward with this? Are you constantly seeking the approval of others before you do something?

Here is the thing. Not everyone is for you. There are those that say they want you to succeed. While they secretly wish and pray for your demise in secret. Therefore, DO YOU!!!!!

Remember, don't let other people's opinions determine your destiny. You don't need anyone's permission to be the person God has created you to be. (Dave Willis)

"For God knew his people in advance, and He chose them to become like His Son, so that his Son would be the firstborn among many brothers and sisters." (Romans 8:29)

NOVEMBER 29

FIX YOUR ATTITUDE

Good days. Bad days. Ugly days. Sad days. Any one of those days can alter your mood and attitude just like that? But should it?

No matter how the wind may blow. Count it all joy for the fiery darts thrown your way. (James 1:2) See, the enemy only comes for you because he knows the blessings that are over your life. If you weren't doing anything he wouldn't touch you. But because you are chosen and God's special treasure, he wants to trip you up. (1 Peter 2:9) DON'T LET HIM!!!!!

Remember, the power of our attitudes is stronger than the power of our circumstances: So, whether you have a "good day" or a "bad day" is entirely up to you. (Dave Willis)

"A joyful heart is good medicine, but a crushed spirit dries up the bones." (Proverbs 17:22)

NOVEMBER 30

THIS IS EMBARRASSING ME

The divorce. The arrest. The bankruptcy. The incident. The breakup. You thought was an embarrassment and was going to cause you to go down. BUT GOD!!!

See, everything that the enemy meant for evil, God is using for your good. (Genesis 50:20) Yes, it hurt and upset you. But it didn't break you.

Remember, your mistakes were not made for the public to bring down. God allowed it to make you stronger. (Derrick Fuller)

"That's why I take pleasure in my weaknesses, and in the insults, hardships, persecutions, and troubles that I suffer for Christ. For when I am weak, then I am strong." (2 Corinthians 12:10)

DECEMBER 1

DON'T GO BROKE IN THIS SEASON

Thanksgiving has come and gone. Which means Black Friday is over with. So, how many folks went on a shopping frenzy buying things that they wanted or thought they needed?

Buying and shopping is all good. Not saying don't shop and spend. However, is it for you or "them"? When you could pay it forward and bless someone who doesn't even have a place to sleep or food to eat. (Proverbs 19:17)

Remember, we buy things we don't need with money we don't have to impress people we don't like. (Dave Ramsey)

"Beware of practicing your righteousness before other people in order to be seen by them, for then you will have no reward from your Father who is in heaven. Thus, when you give to the needy, sound no trumpet before you, as the hypocrites do in the synagogues and in the streets, that they may be praised by others. Truly, I say to you, they have received their reward. But when you give to the needy, do not let your left hand know what your right hand is doing, so that your giving may be in secret. And your Father who sees in secret will reward you." (Matthew 6:1-4)

_____
_____
_____
_____
_____
_____

DECEMBER 2

I NEED OLIVIA POPE

Olivia Pope is a fictional character played by award winning actress, Kerry Washington on the ABC hit Drama series, Scandal. Ms. Pope is a crisis management expert to politicians and power brokers in Washington DC. Ultimately, she is always there to fix someone's problems. So, how many of you need an Olivia Pope?

See, you've had crisis after crisis happen and you don't know what or who to turn to. But you think an Olivia Pope is the answer to your problems?

Remember, sometimes problems don't require a solution to solve them. Instead they require maturity to outgrow them. (Steve Maraboli)

"But if I were you, I would appeal to God; I would lay my cause before him." (Job 5:8)

DECEMBER 3

WHO SAID IT WAS GOING TO MAKE SENSE?

Has "life" been turned upside down and inside out for you? That no matter how hard you try to understand the dysfunction ,it's left you feeling dysfunctional now?

There comes a time that you have to stop trying to figure everything thing out on your own and just trust God. You say you do, but you keep taking matters in your own hands. So, STOP!!!!

Look, God promised that everything would work out. Not that everything makes sense. TRUST HIM!!!! (Dave Willis)

"Trust in the LORD with all your heart, and do not lean on your own understanding." (Proverbs 3:5)

DECEMBER 4

THE COMPANY YOU KEEP

Just because they are your friends doesn't mean they are good friends for you. Be careful of those that you hang around.

There comes a time in your life that you must clean house. So, ask yourself: Do they mean you any good? Are they causing you harm?

Remember, the fact that you can't keep a white garment away from stains, doesn't mean you should sit in the mud. Mind the company you keep, where you sit and stand. Minimize the stain for clean wash. (Moyo Adekoya)

"A man of many companions may come to ruin, but there is a friend who sticks closer than a brother." (Proverbs 18:24)

DECEMBER 5

I MIGHT

Yeah, I might be able to help you. Has someone ever told you that? So, you get your hopes all up only to get let down.

Truth is, it's okay to put your trust in folks. But it's better to but your trust in God.

Remember, you can ALWAYS count on God. He is The Great "I Am" not the "I Might." (Dave Willis)

"It is better to take refuge in the LORD than to trust in people." (Psalm 118:8)

DECEMBER 6

POOR CHOICES

It's not right. It's not fair and you didn't deserve it. YES, revenge seems like the best thing to do. But it doesn't mean it's the right thing. (Exodus 14:14)

No matter what has been done to you, you must know that God has seen it all. EVERYTHING!!! (Hebrews 4:13) And He has promised to handle those that mishandled you.

Remember, people will hurt you. But don't use that as an excuse for your poor choices, use it as motivation to make the right ones. (Lecrae)

'Do not fear them, for the LORD your God is the one fighting for you.' (Deuteronomy 3:22)

_____
_____
_____
_____
_____
_____
_____
_____
_____
_____
_____
_____

DECEMBER 7

BE WHAT YOU'RE LOOKING FOR

Have you ever been looking for something, but the harder you look it seems harder to find? There is a saying, "once you quit looking, you will find it."

No matter what you're trying to find in life, start being in it. Put your words in action! (Proverbs 18:21)

Remember, if you go looking for a friend, you're going to find they're very scarce. If you go out to be a friend, you'll find them everywhere. (Zig Ziglar)

"Say to the righteous that it will go well with them. For they will eat the fruit of their actions." (Isaiah 3:10)

DECEMBER 8

STAY MISERABLE THEN

I need to work out. I need a vacation. I got to eat better. Is that YOU? Are you wanting and wishing, but not doing anything about it?

What are you waiting for?   This is the season that you're going to have to stop talking about it and do something about it!!!!!

Remember, be miserable or motivate yourself. Whatever has to be done, it's always your choice. (Wayne Dyer)

"A miserable heart means a miserable life; a cheerful heart fills the day with song." (Proverbs 15:15)

DECEMBER 9

WHAT IS MY CHARACTER SAYING?

In life, you're going to have circumstances that are going to happen to you that will be out of your control. Yes, some of the things that might have happened could've been at the result of someone's action.

But just because they acted a fool doesn't mean that you should stoop to their level. Truth is, God is going to take care of you and them. It is well!

Remember, your character should always be stronger than your circumstances. (Dave Willis)

"More than that, we rejoice in our sufferings, knowing that suffering produces endurance, and endurance produces character, and character produces hope, and hope does not put us to shame, because God's love has been poured into our hearts through the Holy Spirit who has been given to us." (Romans 5:3-5)

DECEMBER 10

IT BROKE MY HEART

Have you ever been through something so bad that you had no idea how you were going to come from it?   BUT GOD!!!

See, life might have dealt you some crushing blows, but you're still standing. Truth is, had you not have gone through that, you wouldn't be where you are today. (Genesis 50:20)

Remember, what breaks your heart is part of a divine design to bring change! (Andy Stanley)

"We are hard-pressed on every side, but not crushed; perplexed, but not in despair; persecuted, but not abandoned; struck down, but not destroyed." (2 Corinthians 4:8-9)

DECEMBER 11

TRYING TO PROVE A POINT

I'm going to tell them how I feel. Actually, I ain't saying nothing. Is that you? Are you trying to prove a point?

Life and death are in the power of the tongue. (Proverbs 18:21) You have the very thing in you that can cut someone down or build them up. So, what do you choose?

Remember, every word has consequences. Every silence too. (Jean Paul Sartre)

"When there are many words, transgression is unavoidable, But he who restrains his lips is wise." (Proverbs 10:19)

DECEMBER 12

WHICH CAT ARE YOU COPYING?

I want to be like her. I look up to him. I wish I could have what they got. Fact is you don't know the cost of the anointing on someone else's life.

Yes, it might look like it's easy and what they got you want. But be careful of looking up to everybody.

Remember, it's alright to be a copycat if you know which cat to copy. (Jeremiah Wright)

"Beware of false prophets who come disguised as harmless sheep but are really vicious wolves. (Matthew 7:15)

DECEMBER 13

JUSTICE

I've been wronged. Has that, been you? No matter how you look at, it's not right and it ain't fair.

Sometimes things aren't what they appear to be. Vinegar looks like water until you taste it and then you will be in for a treat.

Don't trip because he or she hasn't gotten what they deserve yet. Fact is, that's not for you to worry about anyways. God got this!!!! (Deuteronomy 32:35)

Remember, justice is not something God has. Justice is something that God is.   (A.W. Tozer)

"When justice is done, it brings joy to the righteous but terror to evildoers." (Proverbs 21:15)

DECEMBER 14

LET THEM REMAIN FOOLS

Trying to talk to a person who is stubborn and stuck on not changing, is just like talking to a brick wall. You will be doing all the talking and nothing is going to change from the wall. It will remain the same.

Just because a person wants to remain foolish doesn't mean that you should get on their level. It's a fool that gives full vent to their spirit, but it's the wise that holds it back. (Proverbs 29:11)

Remember, you can give a person knowledge, but you can't make them think. Some people want to remain fools, only because the TRUTH requires CHANGE! (Tony A. Gaskins Jr.)

"The fear of the LORD is the beginning of knowledge, but fools despise wisdom and instruction." (Proverbs 1:7)

DECEMBER 15

THE WRONG TRAIN

Let's face it, life happens. There are things that will happen to you that will occur that you will have no way of expecting.

However, just because you didn't see it coming doesn't mean that God didn't. Fact is, you don't have to panic or freak out about it. (Jeremiah 29:11)

So, just because it didn't go the way you thought, doesn't mean that God doesn't have a Ram in the bush. (Genesis 22:13)

Remember, if you board the wrong train, it is no use running along the corridor in the other direction. (Dietrich Bonhoeffer)

"Beloved, do not be surprised at the fiery trial when it comes upon you to test you, as though something strange were happening to you." (1 Peter 4:12)

DECEMBER 16

THE INEVITABLE AND THE CHOICE

Tell me the bad news first. Well, just give me the good news now. Is that you? Would you rather be hit with the good, bad or ugly in the open?

Here is the thing. No matter how it comes, it's going to come. There is no way to escape the disappointments that life will bring. However, how you react to them is what matters.

Remember, disappointments are inevitable. Discouragement is a choice. (Charles Stanley)

"They do not fear bad news; they confidently trust the LORD to care for them." (Psalm 112:7)

DECEMBER 17

WHO ARE YOU IN THE DARK?

It's easy to put on the facade around everyone. However, the true test is what you do and who you are behind closed doors.

The question you need to ask yourself is: Who am I at home and in public? Is your representation always at work or are you the same, no matter what?

Remember, character is what a man is in the dark. (Dwight L. Moody)

"To open their eyes and turn them from darkness to light, and from the power of Satan to God, so that they may receive forgiveness of sins and a place among those who are sanctified by faith in me.'" (Acts 26:18)

DECEMBER 18

A ROCKING CHAIR

There is a saying that says: Why worry if you're going to pray. Why pray if you're going to worry. So, why are you?

Quit stressing yourself out about something out of your control. At the end of the day, what YOU can do is one thing. And what God can do is another.

Remember, worry is like a rocking chair. It requires a lot of effort, but it doesn't get you anywhere. (Erma Bombeck)

"Do not be anxious about anything, but in everything by prayer and supplication with thanksgiving let your requests be made known to God." (Philippians 4:6)

DECEMBER 19

CROSSING MONKEY BARS

Painful experiences can cause hurt, trauma and depression. No matter what the root, the cut can still ache.

But just because the aftermath might have left you in pain; doesn't mean that you must stay there. It's time to heal and let go. (Psalm 147:3)

Remember, getting over a painful experience is much like crossing monkey bars. You have to let go at some point in order to move forward. (C.S. Lewis)

"Brothers and sisters, I do not consider myself yet to have taken hold of it. But one thing I do: Forgetting what is behind and straining toward what is ahead," (Philippian 3:13)

DECEMBER 20

AT THE END OF THIS

I get it. You're tired, frustrated, drained and more than that you're sick and tired of being sick and tired.   BUT GOD!!!!

See, the enemy wants you to give up and throw in the towel and say, that's it I'm done! But oh no!!!!! That's when you must fight the hardest because the tide is about to shift. (Ephesians 6:10-18)

Remember, don't you give up. Don't you quit. You keep walking. You keep trying. There is help and happiness ahead... It will be all right in the end. Trust God and believe in good things to come. (Jeffrey R. Holland)

"So, let's not get tired of doing what is good. At just the right time we will reap a harvest of blessing if we don't give up." (Galatians 6:9)

DECEMBER 21

GOD DON'T CHANGE

I like you. I love you. I hate you. I can't stand you. Sound familiar? Well, that's how some folks are. Wishy washy.

Truth is, they might be with you today but tomorrow gone. But God will always be with you no matter what. (Deuteronomy 31:6)

Remember, though our feelings come and go. God's Love for us does not. (C.S. Lewis)

"For I *am* the LORD, I change not;" (Malachi 3:6)

DECEMBER 22

YESTERDAY'S JUNK

The definition of junk is "old or discarded articles that are considered useless or of little value". Truth is we all have junk in our lives that need to be removed. A lot of times, it's not always items. Some people need to go as well.

Today, you need to do some evaluating and clean house. Throw out the things that are taking up space.

Remember, you can't reach for anything new if your hands are full of yesterday's junk. (Louise Smith)

"For I am about to do something new. See, I have already begun! Do you not see it? I will make a pathway through the wilderness. I will create rivers in the dry wasteland." (Isaiah 43:19)

_____
_____
_____
_____
_____
_____
_____
_____
_____
_____

DECEMBER 23

TIRED OF REJECTION

You step out on faith time and time again and you still get rejected. Now because of the rejection you don't trust. You have a wall up surrounding your heart and you've become cold.

But thank God, we know the devil is a lie!!!! Truth is, you might have gotten rejected. But that rejection was God's protection. And He is with you and seeing you through, even when you feel alone. (Isaiah 41:10)

Remember, God will never reject you. Whether you accept Him is your decision. (Charles Stanley)

"Coming to *Him*, a living stone, indeed rejected by men, but chosen *and* precious in the sight of God," (1 Peter 2:4)

DECEMBER 24

TEMPORARY PLEASURE, BUT PERMANENT REGRET

It feels good and looks good, but it isn't good for you. However, you keep going back.

Unfortunately, that's how a lot of folks operate. The things that are bad for you will give you the pleasure that you desire. But just because it gives you pleasure doesn't mean that there won't be consequences to them.

Remember, never trade temporary pleasure for permanent regret. (Dave Willis)

"But the one who lives for pleasure is dead, even while she lives." (1 Timothy 5:6)

DECEMBER 25

IT'S MORE THAN CHRISTMAS PRESENTS

CHRISTMAS DAY

Merry Christmas!!! That is what you're going to hear all day long. It's Christmas time, so why not be merry and full of cheer. Folks are giving and receiving gifts today. However, there is one special gift that we should not forget this morning.

Today is the day we honor and celebrate Jesus Christ's birth. Christ died for you and me. (Romans 5:8) Presents are nice, and we love them. But how many of you want the presence of God more than the earthly presents you receive? The gift of God is eternal life in Christ Jesus Our Lord. (Romans 6:23)

Remember, gifts make all of us happy. But it's that long lasting gift - a relationship with God - that's better than anything!

"For to us a child is born, to us a son is given, and the government will be on his shoulders. And he will be called Wonderful Counselor, Mighty God, Everlasting Father, Prince of Peace." (Isaiah 9:6)

DECEMBER 26

FOLKS KEEP LETTING ME DOWN

Getting your hopes up only to be dropped and let down can hurt to the core. Your gut told you, "do not trust," but you thought this time would be different.

Fact is, folks can let you down all-day long. They can make a promise and not keep it. But God is not like man that He shall lie. If He promises you and said it; He will do it!!! (Numbers 23:19)

Remember, any fool can count the seeds in an apple. Only God can count all the apples in one seed. (Robert H. Schuller)

"It is better to take refuge in the Lord than to trust in man." (Psalm 118:8)

DECEMBER 27

DO THE RIGHT THING

I should have said something. But only if I would have stepped up. Has that been you before? You knew the right thing to do but you failed to do it?

One of the hardest things to do is the "right thing." You shouldn't do what society wants, family or friends. But it's up to YOU to decide. What's the right thing?

Remember, if you start today to do the right thing, you are already a success, even if it doesn't show yet. (John C. Maxwell)

"Learn to do what is good. Seek justice. Correct the oppressor. Defend the rights of the fatherless. Plead the widow's cause." (Isaiah 1:17)

DECEMBER 28

I'VE RUN OUT OF CHEEKS

That's okay, just turn the other cheek. Sound familiar? Are you tired of turning your cheek, time and time again because of fools?

YES, it ain't right. But don't let others change YOU. God saw it all and will avenge those that have come against you. It's not for you to worry about it. But you must stand in faith and trust Him. (Romans 12:19)

Remember, weak people revenge. Strong people forgive. Intelligent people ignore. (Albert Einstein)

"But to you who are listening, I say: 'Love your enemies, do good to those who hate you, bless those who curse you, pray for those who mistreat you.' If someone slaps you on one cheek, turn to them the other also. If someone takes your coat, do not withhold your shirt from them. (Luke 6:27-29)

DECEMBER 29

REALLY GOD?

Do you ever find yourself asking God, "Really God?" I mean your life has been so crazy that even Lifetime couldn't write this type of script.

Fact is, this is the plan. And God knew it all the time. (Jeremiah 29:11) It might seem crazy to you and you wish that it would all go away. But you must be still....Wait patiently for Him and just watch the deliverance of The Lord on your behalf. (Exodus 14:13)

Remember, does God guarantee the absence of struggle? NOT IN THIS LIFE......But He does pledge to reweave your pain for a higher purpose. (Max Lucado)

"The *One* comforting us in all our tribulation, for us to be able to comfort those in every tribulation through the comfort with which we ourselves are comforted by God." (2 Corinthians 1:4)

DECEMBER 30

THE GREATEST MISTAKE YOU'LL MAKE

I want to do it, but I'm scared. What if I fail? She might say no. What if he rejects me? Sound familiar to you? Truth is, God doesn't give us a spirit of fear. (2 Timothy 1:7)

Everything that you want to do God has given you the power and authority over. (Luke 10:19) You can't live in fear to the "what if's" in life. What if you didn't do it?

Remember, the greatest mistake we make is living in constant fear that we will make one. (John C. Maxwell)

"So, do not fear, for I am with you; do not be dismayed, for I am your God. I will strengthen you and help you; I will uphold you with my righteous right hand." (Isaiah 41:10)

DECEMBER 31

IT'S GORGEOUS AT THE END

Change and new beginnings can be challenging. The enemy can creep in your head and make you doubt, fearful and weary. But that's why he's a lie!!! (John 8:44)

Truth is change isn't a bad thing. You must forget what was and embrace what God is doing in the NOW. (Isaiah 43:19)

Remember, real change is difficult at the beginning, but gorgeous at the end. Change begins the moment you get the courage and step outside your comfort zone; change begins at the end of your comfort zone. (Roy T. Bennett)

"Brothers and sisters, I do not consider myself yet to have taken hold of it. But one thing I do: Forgetting what is behind and straining toward what is ahead," (Philippians 3:13)

ABOUT THE AUTHOR

Travasa Holloway- Buford is a Henderson, Kentucky native and resides now in Mobile, Alabama. She is the proud mother of Ra'Mon aka Ray & Rod Holloway. She has been in advertising for over 20 years and is currently the Digital Media Manager for a station cluster including: Urban AC WDLT; News/Talk WXQW-A; Top 40 WABD; Urban WBLX and Gospel WGOK-A.

She is a member of **Eagles' Nest Ministries Church** under the leadership of **Bishop Daniel J. Richardson**, where she oversees the Media Ministry. She also handles the Media Ministry for her home church that she is close with in Evansville Indiana, **New Hope Missionary Baptist Church** under the leadership of **Pastor Rabon L. Turner Sr.**

Travasa is very active in the community by mentoring young girls and speaking with women that are going through various trials and storms. She also writes daily Devotionals that reach thousands of people every day from her ministry, **TNHB Inspirations, LLC**.

Contact/Bookings, Email: tnhb.inspirations@yahoo.com

www.ingramcontent.com/pod-product-compliance
Lightning Source LLC
Chambersburg PA
CBHW071232290426
44108CB00013B/1380